JOURNEY INTO THE NEW MILLENNIUM

TRANSMISSIONS FROM SIRIUS

By Clairvoyant Wendy Munro

TRIAD

For information address:
TRIAD Publishers Pty.Ltd.
P.O. Box 731
Cairns
Qld. 4870, Australia
Ph: (070) 930 121
Fax: (070) 930 374

Book Title:
Transmissions From Sirius - Journey Into The New Millennium

Author:
Wendy Munro

National Library Of Australia: ISBN: 0 646 23473 0
Printed in Australia

Triad publications aim at aiding and inspiring
a spiritually unfolding humanity.

Acknowledgements

It is always with gratitude that I look back at the people who have influenced my life and helped me to believe in myself. Without their encouragement I would not have had the confidence to proceed with this book.

I would like to thank both Tobi and Teri Weiss of Power Places Tours for their support and encouragement and the confirmation of the Sirian message. Without the opportunities they gave me, I would not have known my capabilities.

I especially thank Barbara Hand Clow who took me beyond myself. Her complete faith in my ability to reach and stretch into unknown realms was overwhelming. She knew me more than I knew myself. I love you, Barbara. Thank you.

My very special thanks to Zara Bellett. Her continual encouragement and dedication to support the birthing of this book enabled it to happen. Zara transcribed thousands of pages of channelled information and then assisted me in arranging volumes of information into a format that touches the soul, enabling this book to happen. Thank you Zara, for your patience and your commitment.

Thank you also Lazaris. You have been my great love since 1985. Without your love and inspiration and your confidence in me as a writer, this book would not have been written. The information that you have given has flowed into my very blood and has changed me beyond measure. Lazaris, you have shown me the love of Goddess and the true meaning of Sirius. Thank you for always being there.

I would also like to thank all my special friends for their encouragement and especially my two sons, Aaron and Kristen, who have coped with a mother who was always preoccupied. I am grateful for their levels of awareness that have enabled them to understand the greater picture.

CONTENTS

Author's Foreword

My ability to see beyond the mundane world was always a mixed blessing. As I attempted to cope, as a child, in a third-dimensional world that I mostly feared, my other world spiritual family was my main source of love and support. Many times I prayed to my angelic friends to take me home. Their smiles of love spoke of a purpose; that I was being prepared for a destiny they promised to support. They spoke to my heart in different ways. I learned to distinguish between those who belonged to Earth and those who came from far beyond. I saw the light which flowed from their very essence.

When my father died, I opened to a new dimension of 'seeing'. I began to see the discarnate beings who had already recently passed away and discovered I could talk to them. I soon learned how to follow the guidance of my spiritual family and they took me on many journeys, both in the unseen realms and also in the physical world. I was taken beyond the great void into worlds of light and worlds of darkness. I was shown destruction and annihilation. I was told Earth was not to be destroyed and many were working toward that end. I was to assist in raising the consciousness of humanity.

Travelling around the physical world initiated a vivid recall of previous lives lived at times of major change. I was reawakening, as well as confirming for myself the information given to me.

Well trained for the role I was to play, I had been a nurse, medical laboratory technologist, physiologist and metaphysician in this life. In previous lifetimes I have been a priestess, healer, alchemist, prophet, oracle and scribe. It is now my task to be the mediator. As a clairvoyant, channel, prophet, oracle and scribe I commit myself to the service of a humanity in transition toward wholeness, light and love.

There comes a time when the heart's desire is greater than the resistance to express. This book had to be birthed. The Sirians had waited patiently until I was ready. I found it easy to open for the Sirian information to flow through me, although the labour was long and I was taken through many countries until I was ready to believe their message. They spoke through me in England, America, Egypt, Peru and Greece. They gave me information only they could know. They proved to me many times over the validity of the information. As a scientist I needed proof each time. They gave me even more visions, opened my eyes even wider to a world beyond physicality. I was moved to tears and overwhelmed at the accuracy of their revelations.

My support team was ready and waiting. All I had to do was say '*yes*'. It is easy to say 'yes' when you are ready and when it is the right time. In the writing I grew and went through my own transformation. I have been channelling since the mid 1970's. It was not an easy path during the early stages. However, at all times, the love of the Sirians encouraged me and kept me focussed. I have seen and received messages and confirmation from so many sources it would be beyond the scope of this introductory note to mention them all by name. There was Jesus, Melshizedek, Moses, Kuthumi, Serapis, several of the disciples and many of the great philosophers and physicians from ancient Greece and Egypt. I felt their love and wisdom and knew at all times without doubt we as humanity would succeed in the healing and transformation of our planet. It is my task to give the message of hope and encouragement and to show the way.

Introduction

Know this beloved children, you have travelled a great journey. You have been travelling for aeons of time. Much of that period of recent times had been in the dark and you have only had the shadows and the reflections to guide your footsteps.

This lifetime is the lifetime in which you will feel the shadows coming to life, for this lifetime has the potential to be the last lifetime you will ever experience in this third-dimensional expression. The electromagnetic fields of energy, around and through you and your planet will be of such magnitude that you will be changed, never to return again to that third-dimensional expression.

You will begin again to experience the joy and the fun of being a co-creator in this drama, this play of life. You have given yourself a beautiful gift, to be here in this life, at this period of time. Hold fast to the positive visions of your future. Go within and find and maintain your centre. While it appears at times as if there is tragedy and trauma, to the degree that you are able to remain centred you will keep yourself and your planet on course and you will keep your future and your destiny in harmony with the Great Plan which you all came to fulfil.

This time you will realise miracles. This time you will transform yourself beyond measure and find the way to the Truth you have been seeking, the Light of all lights, the wonder that is able to produce and perform miracles. Yes indeed, you will change water into wine. You will know and you will understand the truth and mystery behind all Truths, that you too are like the Spirit that flows through your own veins. You too are in truth, the Essence and the Chalice. You are the one who carries the Light of all lights within every cell of your being. You are the ones who will come forth in this life to perform the miracles of all time. Yes, you too will create miracles of healing. We are here to find a way to penetrate into the very depths of your hearts so that you may be reminded again that you are not alone, and that your journey will be rich, full, and abundant and prosperous in every way.

Allow your hearts and your souls to be uplifted, such that you will sing the praises of that which you truly are. We thank you for your love and for your willingness to take that step. Allow your hearts to be opened. Allow your light to shine. Allow yourself to perceive and receive the wisdom of all ages. You are the creators of a new future, a new time, and you are now here in order to do just that.

Embrace yourselves and be embraced by our love. We surround you and we have surrounded you throughout all times, for we have existed throughout all times and so too have you. The only difference is that we are aware of that premise and you have yet to become aware. We have transcended time and space and so too will you, yet you will do it in a very different way. You will achieve mastery in a way that is totally new. We will be here to applaud and encourage you as you take those first steps in your transformation and your metamorphosis.

Brothers and sisters, we have walked this path together. We have stood in each other's shadow, certainly so, for none is more than the other. We have visited you in your dreams. We have taught you in the Sacred schools that lie beyond your Earth plane and beyond the mists of time and space. We have travelled with you in your dream body to those places beyond the mists so that you may meet again with those who are your spiritual family. In past times we have studied together and now we share again a great journey and a great adventure that will take us into a new world and a new spirituality.

We are the Sirians. We have walked with you through ages of time and have again returned to assist you in this your greatest transformation. We have appeared in many guises, yet always at times of change and transformation when it was necessary for you to receive the tools appropriate for the next stage of your journey. We will discuss ourselves more fully as we proceed in our communications together.

There is a great light entering your world: a light that holds the love of God/Goddess. Throughout time we have always aligned ourselves with Her great love. We have always appeared in your world when she was to be honoured and recognised. You may know us as Ishtar. We carry the light and love of God/Goddess into the world and

2

it may be a beacon to show the way home. We will speak as a plural energy for in that respect we embrace the composite of the feminine energy. We have been known by many names throughout time, even as Isis. We have come to speak at this time to prepare the way, to assist you to open your hearts to receive the great gift from God/Goddess. Your responsibility is to receive this gift. As you become the receivers thus will the doors of destiny be revealed to you.

Chapter I
The Great Adventure

CHAPTER ONE

The Great Adventure

Your Earth is moving and growing as it never has before. You as a humanity are evolving as your planet grows. You are remembering a time in your distant past in a land called Lemuria when you made a decision to participate in the evolution and transformation of a humanity into its full expression of spirituality. You decided to participate in a great adventure which involved the creation of a new world and a new species. Through many ages you have been preparing for just this life. For thousands upon thousands of years you have moved through the stages of the child and the adolescent and now you have come of age. You are now ready to move into a virgin future of your own creation.

In the past you have experienced lifetimes in other worlds, civilisations of a different kind. In some of those lifetimes you were humanoid, in others you were not. Some of those worlds ended, some evolved. On your own planet Earth you have also been practising and experimenting. Atlantis was one such example, and so too was Lemuria. Atlantis was an ending with such disastrous consequences that you fell to the third dimension and back into the dark ages. You lost all connection with the higher dimensional beings. We were no longer able to communicate with you in the way we had before. We had to wait until you were ready. After a sufficient period of time we again appeared to you and became your teachers. Now you are ready to take up the challenge that was the choice given to you. You are now poised on the brink, ready to give birth to yourself. You are your own midwife on a mystical adventure giving birth to a new world and a new spirituality. You are doing what has never been done before. You are evolving a new world and transforming a humanity with full consciousness.

You have made the decision to participate in a conscious transformation that will expand your awareness beyond the third-dimensional limitations of time and space into the multiple dimensionality of your universe. The decision to allow this to happen was not taken lightly and intervention was needed. You have been given permission and now you are about to create a totally new spiritualised humanity. You are finding the way to ascend. This will require a total metamorphosis. Your body is already experiencing some of the changes. In the process of your transformation you will discover a very powerful principle. You are a creator of your world and of yourself. You are waking up to your potential. You are becoming the dreamers and the visionaries of a new world. You are to create this new world through your imagination with the power of vision.

Birthing yourself

You are giving birth to yourself in a very different way, a very profound way. It is in some respects a long and enduring birth, yet in other respects it will feel as if the intensity of that birth moves in waves like the rhythm of the labour of a mother. It is a pulsation.

At times it feels as if everything in your life is moving along just fine, then all of a sudden there is another 'wave', another pressure to encourage you to go deeper, and deeper, and yet even deeper.

Gathered around you are Beings who are encouraging you to go forward into the new world you are creating. Many of you still hold fast to the idea of a world that will be in tragedy and trauma. Many of you believe there will be a continuation of war and conflict. Yet we say you give birth not only to yourself, but also to a new world.

We will give an example. In the Cabalistic ancient scripts is a description of The Gate. It has been termed by many names yet it may be called The Gate Of Life or The Gate Of Death, depending on which way you move through the Gate. For those of you who have come from the light and the awareness of All through this Gate, you will interpret it as the Gate Of Death because it confines and restricts you in this limited third-dimensional form.

We would interpret it as The Gate Of Life, The Gate Of Awakening. In past times when you have died you lost consciousness at the moment of your death. You have gone through the transition of dying without the awareness, without the consciousness of going through the Gate.

In your Bible it says you will go through the Pearly Gates. Why would they call them the Pearly Gates? The pearl is a feminine symbol likened unto the moon. It is simply the reflection or mirror of your soul. Each and every one of you, when you go through that Gate, will see the mirror, the image, the reflection of yourself. We are sure you have heard of, and some of you may have even experienced, a near-death experience. At the point of almost dying your life passes quickly before your eyes. At that point of death, some will say you pass before the Judgement Seat. It is more that you will pass through the Gate Of Pearl where you will see the image, the reflection, of the life you have lived and you will become the assessor, the determiner, of that which you have experienced in your life.

We are telling you this because you are going through this gate into a greater life, into a greater expression of yourself, and as you pass through the gate this time, *you may remain conscious*. Already you are beginning to reassess your life and determine for yourself "What do I need to change about the way I am expressing myself?" "What is that way of expressing that is no longer appropriate?"

Oh yes, in the past you would pass through the Gate Of Death and you would pass before the Judgement Seat (and we use this metaphorically speaking) and there would be the karmic Masters who would assess and determine for you whether you lived the life you had chosen to live. And you would realise "Oh, my goodness, oh, I was a judger. I was very critical!" And you would determine whether or not you did have the right approach to life and what you needed to change.

We tell you this because you are creating that very same experience *now* in your life. You are moving *consciously* through the Gate, the narrow gate, into those other dimensions, yet before you go, you must pass through that narrow opening in order to determine: "Is there anything that I still need to release, to change, before I give birth to myself through the Gate, that New World I will be born into consciously?"

This period of time in your life is one you have never experienced before. It is totally new, totally different. The veils will be removed and all that has been obscured and obstructed will begin to clear in order for you to vision again in new ways.

We are now encouraging you, as you begin this process of going through this birth, to realise the power of image. We wish to stress this if we may, so you may understand that in your brain you have a number of portions that may be called the frontal lobes, the hypothalamus, the thalamus. You have various other organs that come together, such as the pineal gland to release various chemicals and hormones such as polypeptides, neuropeptides, which in their own particular way respond to image. There will be a chemical reaction as a response to your ability to image. We have spoken somewhat in the past and we will speak again, perhaps a little more explicitly, for this is such an important pattern that you need to embrace at this time.

The pineal gland

You have within your brain, an eye. It is known now as your pineal gland. Perhaps some of you have called it the third eye. We are not necessarily referring to the third eye as you understand the third eye to be. In the past times, so many hundreds of thousands of years ago, this eye was large - so very large. It was approximately the size of a large walnut inside the brain. This organ was light sensitive and it was also the means whereby each individual was able to maintain the connection to its Source. It had many functions, most of which are now only evident in a new-born baby, but because the baby cannot communicate you are not able to determine their experiences in relationship to yours. This was a very large sensory organ that caused a protrusion at the crown of the head. The remnants of that larger sized organ may be seen in the present as the soft spot, or the warm spot, on the crown of your head. The suture lines of the scalp do not close over this portion of the brain until the child goes through its second separation from its mother from about the age of one to two years.

With the closing of the vortex so many thousands of years ago [more on this later], the connection to the Source was lost and that sensory organ began to diminish in size and function. Alternative pathways for the dendrites and the axons were created inside the brain. That portion of the brain was closed down, subsequently denying that eye the activations that were so important and necessary for its ability to function in the way for which it was originally intended. As a result of its inactivity, as a result of the decision not to see, [and we use the word 'see' in multiple ways here, e.g. "I don't want to know. I don't want to be enlightened."] that organ gradually became smaller and smaller until now it is perhaps the size of a pea, perhaps a little larger for some of you.

Now the time has come when you are beginning the recalibration of those pathways, the reactivation of the dendrites and the axons to open up and develop the ability to see again.

Many of you feel and sense the pulsing of the crown of your head. Have you noticed? Those of you who make the decision "I wish to see! I want to know more! I want to learn! Let me know! Tell me more! I want to reach, stretch and grow!", it is you who are creating that activation. In your decision to move into a future that you can envision, that you can image, or imagine, the very act of imagining activates those pathways!

Ishtar describes the pineal gland

With the influence of the God/Goddess energy, the pineal gland is activated. You used to have a little antenna which is your pineal gland. It is truly your third eye, not the pituitary. The pineal gland used to protrude through the crown of your head. It was light sensitive at a time when sunlight did not penetrate through the mists that surrounded your planet. It was such a very long time ago. You were not as you are now, certainly not. So, at that period of time, there was a gland like an eye, a very different type of eye than the two that have evolved for a different purpose. This particular eye responds to a different light. It responds to the light of God/Goddess. As every child recognises its mother, so too will you recognise and respond to the light from God/Goddess.

This energy has a very high fine vibration that will ultimately draw all of humanity into resonance with it. Initially, God/Goddess has the task of activating the brain so that it can function according to a prerecorded program to assist the evolution of the human form. Ultimately it will change the DNA.

The process of transformation is a co-operation between the light of God/Goddess and the individual person.

Your whole body is now being infused with light. As it flows through into the cells of your body, the light from which the cells are made is activated, and the memories you have brought with you begin to surface. You will suddenly feel a sense of a new direction, of making new decisions, being more compelled, more impelled, to move forward into something new, something you would not have conceived of doing, even a few months ago. It seems as if suddenly your future has meaning. Your future has purpose and your past experiences seem to lose their control over you. It does not seem to have the same drag; it is as if someone has cut the anchor! How wonderful! The anchor is no longer dragging you back. You no longer look over your shoulders to find out "Who is it this time? Who is holding me back? Is it my mother, my father, my husband, wife, children, my past lives?" Suddenly it seems as if they do not matter any more. What matters is what you intend to do in the future.

As your pineal gland begins to resonate with the light of God/ Goddess it encourages you to change direction. Instead of looking to your past as the cause you will now begin to look forward and allow your future to be the reason for your decisions. You are beginning to look up. You are beginning to look forward. You are looking towards the source of light, rather than to the darkness.

12

Yes, we know there were some very powerful times in your past, some very beautiful and some very rewarding. There were some very beneficial times you can certainly draw upon, utilise and integrate with, and take them forward into your future. Those experiences you no longer prefer to remember may be transformed into a positive image to assist in your own healing.

You will enjoy your world as you go beyond 2000. You will have great delight. There will be some beautiful experiences of peace in your hearts and souls as you will have passed through the traumas and dramas that will be present for many, yet may not be part of your own direct experiences. We will be there to assist you as you move through this time of transformation. You only need to ask us when you need guidance or assistance. Every thought you think ripples out in a wave of colour from your brain and from your body. Your thoughts become active in tangible, solid ways which we are able to see. We watch the ripples of colour and we read the continuous streams of like mind and like thought. When we see there is sufficient of like mind and like thought, then we can assist you in bringing about that desire and that dream.

Realise as you move forward there will be the opportunity then for you to meet with those such as ourselves. You will meet us, you will see us, and you will be in many ways like infants that are newborn into a new world. You will need assistance to consciously remember how to interact in those higher dimensional worlds.

Imagine a little baby being born into this physical world. It is helpless and it needs to learn how to function in your physical world. Those Beings who no longer have need of a third-dimensional physical body, are already there waiting, anticipating and expecting you the same as any other parent would be anticipating a new birth. *You are to be born in that higher world, consciously!* The Beings in those other dimensions will be there to assist you in the transitional stages. Even though you may be approximately five or six feet tall, those who have been before you reach to sizes of fifteen to twenty feet in height, depending on the dimensional expression of themselves.

Realise they are waiting with open arms, waiting to assist you to give birth to yourself into that dimension of expression. You will enter into those dimensions with consciousness, with awareness, being able to interrelate using abilities that you will have gained, using skills that you are learning and are going to be learning over the next fifteen to twenty years.

Question: I have a baby seven months old. At that age, do they remember where they have just come from?

The newborn baby can experience many things and we will give you certain factors to consider. The soul of the child will generally enter into the body either at birth, just prior to the birth, or very shortly thereafter. The soul is loosely connected to the body for an initial period of time. Often it is not totally connected to the body until it goes through a process of what you would call baptism or name giving. In the first few days that soul is still very connected to its place of origin, very aware of its connection to its star people. It is able to communicate with them. It is able to see using all of its psychic senses. That child, that newborn baby, sees the auric field with great clarity, sees the spirit world with great clarity and communicates telepathically.

The spiritual support team remains connected to the child and the child is aware of that support during its frequent sojourns into the astral world where it 'dreams', and even in its waking state. Dreaming serves a very important function in stimulating brain pathways and laying down the codes that will later be activated to assist the person to awaken to its purpose in life. The baby also remains very connected etherically and emotionally to its mother. It is connected to such a degree that it has no sense of its own identity as separate from its mother. This separateness does not occur until the child is approximately one and a half to two and a half years of age. The baby or young child identifies with its mother to such a degree that as mother goes through her own traumas, her own joy and excitement, the baby feels that. Each mother giving birth needs to be encouraged to welcome the child with all love, to surround and enfold the child in the embrace of love right from the very beginning.

The initial impact of birth is imprinted on the soul, imprinted on the psyche. That initial imprint is from the very first push of the muscles of the vagina to the very first impression received from the medical, or the support team, at birth. Each and every person present at the birth will have an expression that will imprint on the child, whether it is the doctor who says "This has been a difficult birth" or "What a beautiful child"; the imprint will be there. The imprint is carried forth and is then reactivated at varying stages in the child's life. The first few days of life are absolutely, totally important, so important that it is the karmic activation for the whole of life. The first few days are the imprint for the rest of life.

Question: What happens when there is a forceps delivery?

That is an absolutely traumatic experience for the child. Often, children who have forceps delivery have come into this life to deal with being the victim. They have come into this life experiencing oppression, domination and force. They feel out of control and powerless. As they mature to child and adult, they are often resistant to being told what to do, cannot stand authority figures, and will often be rebellious. They may demonstrate patterns of dependency or co-dependency or become addictive in some way such as alcoholic or workaholic.

That child will often experience, at about the age of fourteen or fifteen, a type of crisis that holds a similar dynamic to their birth, a sense of domination and power that they feel they will need to rebel against. Sometimes this can be a threat to the health. Sometimes it can simply be police interaction, a dominating parent or some other factor that may reactivate that particular trauma. Each child who has had that experience still has the need to resolve that trauma. It simply says that you as humanity have not yet let go of the idea that learning *has* to come through punishment, pain or suffering. You are here to reclaim your power and your willingness to be loved. There will come a time when pain, domination and loss of control will no longer be needed and you will find that delivery at birth will be with ease.

Recalibrating your receptors

Some of you may recall not so very long ago that it was a privilege to have a colour television set in your home. And yes, you were quite content to have black and white television, because it was so new and innovative. Then colour television came. And of course, what do you do with your black and white television set? Why can't you do something with the black and white to make it coloured? What would you do, wear coloured glasses? Why can't you do something to the inner workings of the black and white television? No one has found the way, because you cannot recalibrate a black and white television to make it coloured. You have to buy, or have one given if you are so lucky, a new television set because the calibrations for coloured television are very different from black and white. You may understand that your brains, for the most part, are still functioning in a similar way to the receptors of a black and white television set.

The contrast between enjoying the pleasure of black and white television and the vast difference as you move forward into colour television, is the difference that will occur when you have learned to recalibrate your brain. Then will you see through different eyes, for you will have different receptors [television set] inside your brain.

Over the next several years, the higher frequency light vibration coming through the Sirius vortex will be recalibrating your receptors and will enable you to experience a very different world. The world out there will suddenly take on a new depth, a new dimension, a new vitality, a life that is vastly different from what you are seeing with your present receptors. And the way to activate your colour receptors, if we may so describe them, is to practise the art of imagination. It is in imagining, in imaging, that you will create those pathways that will revitalise that eye that has been dormant for so long. This particular eye not only has the ability to see in the ways in which we have described, but also inter-dimensionally.

There is a story that perhaps many of you have heard. When Magellan sailed into the area of the Pacific Islands, the natives, who had not ever seen a sailing ship and such as he and his men, were absolutely astonished to see these 'gods' step out of nothing into a smaller canoe that rowed to shore. It took the shamans to teach the natives of the islands to be able to see the sailing ship of Magellan.

Equally so, you too will be able to see the equivalent of Magellan ships, not necessarily just flying saucers, you understand. You will also see angelic beings and many other beings that exist in the multidimensional expression that lies beyond your black and white receptors. Your ability to image will activate your ability to see. Yet, along with that, this particular eye, the pineal gland, not only sees in the way your physical eyes see; in the seeing, this eye *knows* for it allows wisdom into its receptors. That particular eye allows in, not only the light of the sun and any other sun in your galaxy or universe; but also the light that comes from God/Goddess and in that activation will come the light that brings the wisdom, the memory and the knowingness of who you truly are.

So we do encourage you to practise imagination, the ability to visualise all things that you would desire to create, both for yourself, those close to you and for your very planet. Use your imagination to find the solutions, whereby you can discover the wisdom and the knowledge that will allow you to see and perceive the greater.

Veils

Soon, very soon, a time will come when the veils that prevent you from seeing will become thinner. It will be a little like when you rise on a winter's day and the mist is strong and heavy on the ground. When the sun rises and the warmth of the sun gradually dissolves the mist, you are able to see beyond the mist to see the beauty of nature.

There was once a dance called The Seven Veils. Each of those veils as danced by the beautiful dancers, represented the veils across the seven chakras. In your physical etheric body, you have veils on each of those levels. Your etheric astral body also has veils.

All of you have physical senses. You take them for granted, until you suddenly have to put on your glasses because your eyes are growing dim, yes? It is the same with your hearing. "Do say that again please. What were you saying? I didn't quite catch it." Your physical senses have been functioning in your life as part of your nature, your God-given gift, as some would say. Now, you also have a set of senses belonging to the other realms. Every realm in which you express yourself has its own senses.

You have been told you will develop your clairvoyant and clair-audient senses. You will become clairsentient, expanding your sense of feeling. Through the olfactory system you will smell more. Your astral body has astral senses and, although we remind you of this, you know it. We know you know it because when you go into your dream state at night and you have a waking dream, or when you come back and remember your dream, you say: "Oh, I had the most wonderful dream last night. I saw that I was...and I hear this...and I smelled and touched that...!" You take it for granted that you are able to see on the astral realms. Then why is it that when you come back into this body you lose the ability to communicate with the astral realms?

Your central nervous system is made up of a spinal column that is made up of a number of nerves, axons, dendrites, the neuronal patterns that move through your brain out into the fingers and toes. These nervous systems, your sympathetic and parasympathetic, behave in such a manner as to be able to give information. And they allow you to have contact with your outer world. If you put your hand on something hot or something cold you are able to give that information to your consciousness. It is your central nervous system that is the mediator between your physical and astral bodies. Your beliefs are stored in the subconscious and those beliefs prevent the flow of information from the astral realms to your conscious mind.

We are not figments of your imagination! We are very real. We are with you! Why can't you see us? We wonder at times just why you can't see us. We do understand you have not yet learned that to be able to see us, you need to have a change within the vibrational frequency of your central nervous system. This will enable the information to flow from the axons, through the synapses into the dendrites, activating various polypeptides, neuropeptides and other chemical stimulants that are needed for the information to be received.

You will need to use specific exercises of the mind and imagination to activate the release of those chemical transmitters. That 'exercise' word really presses your buttons! "I don't want to do that. I want to just sit here and have it happen to me." We wish you to know that participation is involved in all growth processes and it requires your willingness to change those neuronal pathways, to lift the vibrational frequencies. In other words to 'clean the rust from your terminals'. If there is an accumulation at the battery terminals in your car, you would know why the sparks are not flowing and the car is not turning over. You would have to scrape it off. Many of you have accumulations at the end of your terminals. It creates a number of problems and becomes worse as you get older. You wonder why the muscles and bones become decrepit and why you hear grinding sounds. They are deposits between the joints and the ligaments, the tendons.

These deposits accumulate in the nerve endings too, starting from seven years of age. Up until then, a child is generally able to perceive us, to intercept that which is taking place in the inner realms. There are a number of activities which will help you clear those nerve endings. There is often accumulation of toxic deposits, where the little sparks leap across to carry the information. These are caused by beliefs that have been conditioned into each person about the non-existence of other realms and they inhibit the flow of information.

Many of you still hold beliefs conditioned from previous life experiences, added to in your present life; for example, that you have been tortured, burned at the stake, ridiculed in some way, shape or form, because of your ability to be telepathic or clairvoyant, or to have access to wisdom and knowledge from the higher realms. Because of those experiences you decided it is not worth the pain and suffering. You decided this time you will be 'normal'. So you came into this life and created a situation where your mother or father, teacher or priest says: "You must be possessed by the devil! Rubbish child, there is no such thing. It must be your imagination."

Then over time you decide it is not appropriate for you to talk about such things. You build the veils, placing them in position so that type of information is prevented from passing across the synapses into your conscious mind. You no longer see. You no longer hear.

We wish to also remind you of the value of drinking water. Water as you know, is necessary for a battery, is it not? Your battery cannot operate without water. *Your body is a battery!* Have you checked your battery lately? You have a North pole and a South pole, and you have a flow of current that moves through your body. Your nervous system carries the information to tell the vehicle, your body, to respond in certain ways.

We inform you of the value of taking lots of water into your batteries so that you can cleanse the terminals and de-oxidise yourself, as it were. You are also advised to eat only high vibrational foods. Make sure that all you take into your system is of a vibration in harmony with that frequency required to enable your physical body to be cleansed. As well as attending to your physical body you need exercise to detoxify your own lymphatic systems and to strengthen your immune system. Your emotions and your thinking will all change to be in harmony with a higher order. Each of your nerves records information within your subconscious mind. All of your emotions and all of your beliefs are recorded.

It is important you bring your choices and beliefs into harmony with the destiny of your future self. In this way you will be able to create the life you would prefer. It is also appropriate that all your interactions with people are of the highest order. Watch your initial responses in every situation. Let them all come out of love, caring and consideration. Be aware that every thought and word is a vibration.

You are what we would call the farthest extension of the Sacred Word, the Logos made flesh. It is you who are now learning the power of the spoken word, but you are also learning the power of thought. In your thinking you constrict the synapses, causing a dilation or a contraction of the blood vessels, decreasing or increasing the flow of blood into the brain, causing a blockage to the desire for expansion.

You are removing the veils which have existed between your conscious, your subconscious, and instinctive levels. When you sleep at night, you lose consciousness and you enter into that dimension where time and space as you know them change. You move through that veil of forgetfulness and wake up to the dimensional realm where time as you know it does not exist. It alters, it changes. In your waking conscious state you also find the third-dimensional constraints of space and time are changing. There is a gradual change taking place to enable the greater ease of transition between the third dimension and the multi-dimensional worlds. You will become aware of these changes as you observe *the speed of response between the choices you are making for yourself and the manifestation of those choices.*

As you move into fourth and fifth dimensions, you will allow the veils which have protected you from the inundation of all of the memories to be removed. You can then be conscious of all of your lifetimes! How do you become conscious of all of your lifetimes? Remember that you are still in this third-dimensional world, so you are still constrained by time and space. So you have time still spread out in a continuum. You allow time and space to separate your experiences in the same way, as the different channels on your TV set are separated so that you can focus and concentrate. As you become more experienced, you will discover that by a mere shift of focus, you are able to attune to a different dimension in the same way as a turn of the dial tunes you to a different channel. With experience, you will discover how to change the frequency by changing image, emotion, desire, or any other specific code, to access the dimension of past, present or future, even as to past or future lifetimes.

Changes will take place in your own physiology. With the increase in the electrical and the magnetic energies pouring into your planet, these will facilitate a reactivation and a clearing, or the breaking down of the veils that you put in place before you were born.

21

These veils have kept you from seeing beyond this third-dimensional world, have kept you from hearing beyond, have obscured and prevented you from knowing all of those lifetimes. How many times you have asked the question "Why can't I remember my past lifetimes?" So there will be the beginning phases, not totally as yet, but the beginning, as you move forward into the next several years. "Oh, I am starting to get a glimpse. I feel as if someone has pulled the blind up and I have a flash of insight. As if someone has pulled the curtains back." And you will begin to get a glimmer of those decisions that you made suddenly being resolved, no longer being relevant. *You* know about those decisions! "I don't want to see again, because the last time I saw they put me in prison, or they tortured me. I don't want to hear, because when I heard the voices the last time, they burnt me at the stake."

So trust your future, realise that just because it happened in the past does not necessarily mean it will happen in the future. You will begin to go beyond. You will go through the veils of forgetfulness into the light beyond time and space. Your spiritual eyes will *see* and *know*. All that has been obscured will be revealed. You will remember the decisions you have made that have brought you into the depths of a third-dimensional world and you will see the way home.

We encourage you to give yourself an opportunity you have never had before, an opportunity to create the life you want and a world you choose to live in. There are very powerful forces to facilitate you. You are supported in so many ways. You have now come of age. You have now grown up. It is time to take the responsibility firmly and be willing to step forward into your future.

Question: What helps us to stay open, and helps the third eye, the pineal and the pituitary glands?

There are a number of factors that will assist you. One is to be continually aware. There is a tendency for some of you to disappear into a dream state. As you attempt to accommodate this increased energy you will feel as if you are not in your bodies, as if fading out in a sense of vagueness and an inability to be fully present.

Some of you may fall back into old avoidance and withdrawal patterns. When you become aware of yourself doing this, decide to stay conscious. It is important that you bring yourself back to attention. Be attentive. Be focused. Be present. It is important to observe when you are repeating old patterns and determine to change them.

We also suggest practising creative visualisation. Practise imagination. Utilise all of your senses to create those spaces within meditation whereby you can see, smell, taste, touch and hear vividly so you are able to *feel* the touch of feather, and *feel* what it is like to have talcum powder poured on to your hands. *Feel* the touch of water, and feel the difference between water that is cool and water that is warm. Also, in this way, see varying shapes and forms. See them from different angles and move inside them.

Let yourself become a tree; move around the tree. Let yourself become a leaf on the tree. In this way you will be exercising the visualising ability. This will assist you as you move more consciously on to the astral planes when you will use your astral senses, which you would call your clairvoyant and telepathic senses.

You were, so very long ago, unable to feel through your physical bodies. Your nervous system had not extended its nerve endings to the extremities and your legs and arms were not able to feel the sense of touch the way you do now. It needed to develop over time, many hundreds of thousands of years. At the moment you are aware you have two eyes. Originally you did not have two eyes. You had antennae, a little like the antennae on the worms that live in total darkness. You did not have eyes because there was no light. You used the antennae to feel. That is why the sense of feel has now extended through the body.

Eyes developed when light entered your planet. Prior to the light, darkness was upon the face of the Earth. You only needed an antenna. The antenna was your pineal gland. It has since receded very deeply inside the brain. It was an antenna with a vast array of specific abilities which not only perceived shape and texture, but also perceived the varying degrees of shade and light that were just beginning to come through the filter of the dense cloud cover that encompassed your planet. This antenna, this pineal gland, was the source of very high levels of wisdom, for in that very primitive physical form, the wisdom came from a group consciousness shared and distributed equally amongst all who were very early in development. That buried antenna is being activated again in preparation for what will be happening, and what is already happening. The new type of Light which has entered your world will enable that antenna to respond with great wisdom and enlightenment. Pouring into your planet is all the wisdom, all the love and all the light that you will ever need.

Since ancient times it has been known the Sirius vortex would be opened in this period of time, and now, knowing there will be available to you all the wisdom, all the light and all the love, there would be no value in saying "here it is" if you did not have the tools to utilise it. So, along with this gift, your brain is being activated to be the receiver of that new type of energy, that new type of light. With that light comes enlightenment. That eye, the receiver of the new light, is now revealing its secrets and is activating your ability to attune to the broader spectrum of the electromagnetic field.

Pouring down upon your planet, and upon your flesh and bones, is a vibration that will assist you to bring about change. We will see you as a different light, in colour that vibrates in beauty, in harmony and in balance. When we are able to see those colours, we will know it is time for you to be lifted and ushered through the vortex. You will emerge in a new place. When you look to the stars, you will know you have come through. The stars in the sky then will form different patterns and they will shed a new light upon you.

You have heard how the structure of your DNA forms the double helix. It is a wonderful spiral that moves in patterns so precise to create the very foundation of your body. You move through the galaxy in harmony with the greater spiral, weaving, blending, harmonising - the microcosm in the macrocosm.

A new blueprint, that has not been before, is now being established. It holds an image so strong it will cause you to align with it.

This blueprint is a vibrational frequency so high, it is above and beyond anything that can be measured on your planet. Its resonance holds the energy of love and Light. This resonance is moving into the very ventricles inside your brain, creating a wave form that sends messages into portions of your brain that have not been activated before, but have lain dormant waiting for the key of that new blueprint. It will cause an activation within the very circuitry, the neuronic pathways inside your brain, to release neuropeptides and neurotransmitters, which will activate the thalamus, the hypothalamus, the pituitary and the pineal, sending messages into the bloodstream so that the very cells in your body will know how to change.

Those changes began in 1994 and will take from approximately 20 or 30 years to 100 years. Your body will be totally renewed in harmony with the blueprint that has come to your planet. This will allow your bodies to be more able to resonate to the messages that you are receiving. You have been told that by the year 2012 the world as you know it will not be the same. By the year 2012 your bodies will not be the same! *You are physically changing.* The pituitary and the pineal glands are glands that will be activated in very specific ways in the future. Like the lens of an eye, the pineal is the receiver of Light. As you are opening up to the God/Goddess energy and it comes through the crown of your head, you will feel the crown becoming very sensitive.

The crown will soften a little. This is part of the process of change. This energy will create in your brain the changes to enable you to see beyond this physical plane into the fourth-dimensional world. You will know you are in the fourth dimension when you have a conscious communication with the birds, animals and elemental beings from the devic kingdom. When you can see your guides and counsellors as real beings you will know you are right there! There will be no separation! You will see the multitude of inner plane beings as easily as you see your third-dimensional friends. They are waiting for you to see them. They are so very close. Veils have been in the way, preventing you from having face-to-face communication with the great principle of love and light. There are shadows within you still in the way. The shadows will need to have more light shed upon them. God/Goddess in her wisdom is now shining forth upon you. One of her purposes in your life is to reactivate the pineal gland, to become once again that organ of receptivity, to become again that light receiver and transmitter sending light throughout the body so the body may be transformed.

Yes, this pineal gland is opening again so you may 'see'. It is not seeing with your third-dimensional eyes, although you will also be using those in a very different way. The inner eye is an eye that is primed to image and imagination. This eye carries the image in the same way as a hologram carries a three-dimensional image; so real, that you can step into it, taste it, touch it, smell it and feel it! When this eye is activated within your brain and you use it as it was meant to be used, an organ of image and light, an organ of enlightenment in the true sense of what enlightenment means, this organ will create those three-dimensional images that will have their connection to the multi-dimensional universe.

We are so excited!! We are able to see these multi-dimensional images being portrayed, similar to when you go to the theatre. The screen in front of you has a projector which projects the images onto the screen. You are projecting your images into the screen of the universe and we see them. Oh yes, it is more exciting than going to the movies! These images come together in a way of frequency resonance. Like blends with like. Each frequency finds its own and blends together. Thus you become the creators of your world. That is the reason why, when a group of people hold an image and project the image into the atmosphere, into the hologram, it is then experienced and manifested in the way in which we said happens so quickly now. When there is political unrest, then there will be devastation to represent that unrest very quickly.

Through the activation of image, your pineal gland, an organ of image, releases in its awakening an essence or elixir that has the task of transforming you. You take it for granted that when you cry, little tears appear in the corners of your eyes. Where do the tears come from? You ask the question but never wait to find the answer. There seem to be so many. The tears flow so abundantly. Your eyes produce the tears. Your inner eye also releases a fluid. It is a fluid of a different kind, released whether you visualise a joyful image or one of trauma, tragedy or fear. It will release an essence, an elixir, that is in harmony with the image it creates.

It is wise, is it not, for you to maintain images of ecstasy and love, images that create the idea of a future that will be beneficial to humanity? In the generations to come, this little organ will become larger. It is releasing what is required for a transformation to take place. You are moving forward very rapidly to become that spiritualised human being. Yes, your body is changing.

You will all experience what may be called an internal brain shifting, as it were, on its axis and open up to receive a new type of light. As you become aware of that increased amount of light flowing into your body, as you become aware that the internal brain feels as if it is going through its own changes, and equally so causing those changes to move right down to the cellular level of your body, you will become aware that you will have less need to eat.

Now you will say: "How wonderful! I can lose all that weight!" We would say most of it you do not need anyway, because you are becoming lighter in every sense of the word. Your bodies are becoming lighter because you are taking in more light. You will become lighter because you will not need to carry the extra weight to fasten yourself to this physical planet.

You will become more discerning and sensitive to whatever is detrimental to your body and make more positive choices to lift the resonance of your body so it becomes more of the light body.

Chapter II
Metamorphosis

CHAPTER TWO

Metamorphosis

We would like to use an analogy so you may understand the magnitude of the task you are undertaking. We are aware that so many of you use words without ever exploring the depth of their meaning and the impact they have upon your consciousness. For our analogy we will use the butterfly. Metamorphosis is a total change in shape and form. The caterpillar transforms into the butterfly by creating a chrysalis in which it remains until it emerges fully changed. A number of processes are involved to enable this change to take place. Within the caterpillar's brain certain chemicals are released to facilitate this change. When it emerges it has wings and can fly. In a similar way you too are encased in a chrysalis of your own making. Confined by the limitations of space and time, and a set of beliefs that you continue to maintain from lifetime to lifetime, you keep yourself in your own shell and veil yourself from the possibilities that await you in your future.

Now it is time to set yourself free from your own chrysalis and emerge in your new light body with total awareness. The caterpillar changes into the butterfly with wings that enable it to fly. It is no longer bound, like the caterpillar, limited in its perspective and only able to move slowly from leaf to leaf. It is now able to soar above the flowers and trees and be totally free from its previous limitations in both movement and perspective. So too will you set yourself free, as free as the butterfly. You too, will soar on wings of light and see in ways you have never seen before. Your body will change into a different form. You are now going through your own metamorphosis.

Preparing the body for transformation

The vibrational frequencies of your bodies are increasing. Your bodies are the final frontier. Your body is created out of the densest of

Spirit or light and is the most compact energy. Everything is made of the same substance. There is nothing that is not made of the same one thing. It is only created and expressed in different ways.

Due to the higher vibrational frequencies coming into your planet, your mind is being activated! Very high frequencies of mind activation. Your emotions are also being activated, have you noticed? You are wondering what is wrong with your bodies. "My body feels somewhat strange. Sometimes my body feels tired. Sometimes it feels tense. Sometimes it is toxic. Sometimes I feel as if I am not in touch with my body." This is because your body has not caught up with what is taking place with your mind. So we wish to talk to you about how to allow your body to catch up with your mind, for unless it does, it will let you down when the time comes. "Oh yes, there is the doorway and I wish to go through." "Sorry, but your body is not vibrating at the right frequency!"

We would like to encourage you to begin to look at your body as an extension of your spiritual energy. It is *all* spiritual energy. It is time now to honour your body. Over the next five to six years there will be the potential to develop very serious and life-threatening illnesses and these could be, for example, your lymphatic system becoming very toxic causing you to feel as if you cannot drag your body around; it is becoming so heavy. Some may find an arthritic tendency with inflammation in the joints because you are unwilling to move. "I don't want to move, I don't want to budge. I think I will stay just where I am, thank you very much, yes?" Others may find their digestive system is not functioning very well. "Oh, my intestines, my stomach is not functioning." It is because you do not allow yourself to process all the information that is coming through. You are receiving information, but it is not going anywhere. It stays there *in* your body and you will get the *reactions* in your body.

There will be various other types of illnesses associated with your immune system, your heart, your lungs, your liver. Each of these is relevant in its own way. Each organ is like a doorway. Each organ has a particular function and every function has a vibration. Your liver vibrates at one level and your heart vibrates at another frequency. Everything is synchronised throughout your body. It is like an orchestra and there is a conductor. And who is the conductor? You! Oh yes, and you say "I don't call the tune." Well, not on a conscious level, but there is a very powerful way that you are conducting this orchestra within your body and mostly it is because of the way you think. Many of you hold thoughts that are very destructive to your bodies. We will say destructive to your life, in particular.

Creating the perfect vehicle

Realise you have allowed yourself through various cycles of time to create a physical body. Your physical body in every way, shape and form, is the *perfect* vehicle, the perfect vehicle that is now enabling you to *begin* your journey home.

Over the previous perhaps 250,000 years there has been trial and error in creating your physical vehicle. There was a certain degree of experimentation to discover the right type of physical vehicle that would bring you to this point in time where you could incorporate that light energy to enable you to make this journey home.

We will give you an analogy. Those of you who know a little of your history will realise that in the distant past you did not have motor vehicles. If you wished to travel to distant places you had to plan very carefully, pack the horse and cart, and put all your belongings there and all your provisions and would have to work out how many cycles of the moon it would take before you arrived at your destiny. This needed careful planning and many of you have had those experiences, if you are to believe you have had past lives. Now, as you progressed you realised that the horse and cart was not suitable to go through into the future. You created a more modern, motorised vehicle that allowed you to go the distance in a much shorter time. Equally so, you have found that this physical body is another type of vehicle serving the same purpose to take you from one place to another.

Using the same frame of reference, your physical vehicle has enabled you to begin your life as a baby, and to go through those rapid changes needed by you and accommodated by your body to enable it to be a fitting vehicle. You have moved through many cycles of time to ultimately bring you to the fully completed adult, thence to move through rapid deterioration. The vehicle only served a period of time, approximately 70 to 80 years, perhaps up to 100 years. Again, it has been a process of trial and error to create that perfect physical vehicle to take you to where you wish to go.

We might say, "Well, where do you wish to go?" "Where am I going in this body? I began my life here in this small country town and this is perhaps where I might end my days and they will perhaps bury me within two or three kilometres from where I was born. What have I achieved in the process since birth?" Many, many things. It depends on the individual person, but there is something much more significant taking place. You see, there is something more important at work in the creation of your physical vehicle. *You are now building a prototype model.*

You see those beautiful motor cars, slim and sleek, very sophisticated and electronic in every way; all you need to do is press a button and the little robots inside will take you where you want to go. You link into a central computer, dial up the place you want to go to, sit back in leisurely comfort and the car drives you there. That is already in place in your world. You may not have one of those vehicles yet, but they are certainly available if you have the right amount of money.

Your physical body is on the verge of becoming a prototype model in a similar way to the motor vehicle we have discussed with you. You are just about to put in place the last little bits of programming so that it may, in ease and comfort, take you where you wish to go. It will allow you to move consciously into those other-dimensional experiences that you have lost sight of, lost touch with, through the aeons of time you have been travelling through this planet Earth.

There are certain activities taking place now in the evolutionary pattern. We will give you an illustration. The Aboriginal people in

Australia have remained, for the most part, very true to their original connection to the land, honouring and valuing their particular focus on the land. They have contained within their traditions and beliefs many of the principles they were taught, beyond 60,000 years ago. Those principles, held in secrecy by the elders of the tribes, were nevertheless maintained and handed down by the select few. The Aryan races have no way of accessing and expressing that information and, even if they did, they would not be able to incorporate it into their paradigm because they have a different chromosomal configuration in their brains, and have been conditioned by a scientific paradigm.

The Aboriginal people in Australia and the indigenous people throughout your planet in the distant past, were able to teleport their physical bodies from one place to another. Teleportation was taught in the Mystery schools of Lemuria and it is one of the few abilities that remains within those ancient cultures from those ancient times.

Christ consciousness

Now, it is a specific chromosomal configuration that we wish to discuss with you. There is a concept you understand as Christ consciousness and you understand that as you become Christ conscious, it enables you to perform miracles.

Jesus, the man who walked the Earth, gave you the demonstration of performing miracles. How did he *do* that? Well, he had a chromosomal configuration that was different from yours. You might say: "What was there about that configuration that enabled him to do that and not me? I feel left out, because I cannot change water into wine. I would *love* to be able to change water into wine. I would make a fortune!" His chromosomal configuration allowed him to create exactly what he imagined at the time he desired to create it. It is this ability *you* are moving toward in your evolution!

There was an event that occurred some 90,000 years ago which caused a change in the pathways in your brain. Certain portions of your brain became inactive. We love giving analogies, so forgive us if we divert into an analogy so you may understand.

Some of you, in your country towns, may find that the Main Roads Department may decide in its wisdom to change the position of the main road through town. As a result of that, certain businesses which were previously connected to the main road would suddenly find they had lost business. They become very irate. "I used to have a passing traffic. Now you have changed the main road to over there, and no one comes into my business any more!" Well, that is what happened to your brain!

There were those little brain cells which had this wonderful business, and had incredible abilities, supplying much to the skills of the person who had those abilities, and suddenly, the Main Roads Department changed the configuration of the roadworks within your brain. As a result, the passing traffic no longer passed through those brain cells and they were out of business. Now, those brain cells which were out of business were the ones that were specifically designed to allow you to be clairvoyant, to allow you to be telepathic, to allow you to have abilities that you lost along the way, during those thousands of years. They are amazing!

Now, the Main Roads Department, in its wisdom, has said: "Well, we have now realised the error of our ways. We will now change the road system back to where it was." As a result of that, those portions of the brain that had been inactive during that period of time, are now being reactivated. Does that mean you will become clairvoyant again and clairaudient? Certainly so! Each one of you! "Oh, but I do not wish to. I will hide under a rock and not be part of that process of change." Can you hide from the light of God/Goddess? You cannot. Having said that, in the realisation that you are now activating new pathways so the business of opening up to those new abilities can develop, there is something else that needs to be acknowledged. Let us use our imagination for a moment.

When the Main Roads Department moved the roads, the areas of the old business sector became dilapidated. They lost interest in their businesses and forgot to water the plants. They forgot to paint the roofs and forgot to wash the windows. They looked somewhat drab.

In a similar way, you too have forgotten to polish the windows of your own spirituality. You have forgotten to paint the walls, so to speak, and to sweep away the cobwebs. Those of you who may decide to leave, can give yourselves the opportunity to be born into a new body and still be a part of the transformation and ascension. You will realise the importance of going home consciously. It is only a short time before the transition takes place. Some of you will choose to do it in this lifetime. We have said to you the new roadworks are beginning. The activation of those portions of the brain will allow the release of certain neurotransmitters and chemicals, which will allow a transformation to take place within the cellular level of the body, and then you will see many miracles taking place, and *you can* be one of those miracles. It is necessary for you to care for yourself, to go about the business of improving your life, your body, and your relationships with yourself, with those close to you and with that of the highest Order.

There is within each of you a genetic pattern which was chosen, even before this planet Earth existed, even before the physical form that you are now inhabiting, experiencing and expressing through, existed. Those genetic codes and those patterns were preformed. They were the original blueprint of what was to be the fulfilment, the destiny and the purpose of the ultimate human form. Be aware that the evolutionary pattern, the code that has been pre-established even as the blueprint before physical form existed as it is now, is in the stages of preparing the mind and preparing the brain for the next stage of the transformation. The brain is a futuristic instrument within your physical body. Your brain is also pre-coded. It is unfolding and will continue to unfold.

Those on the higher levels, who are aware of the changing human form, realise that the form you are presently occupying cannot carry itself through to the destiny that is pre-planned by you as physical beings without becoming spiritualised. So you are preparing the way, giving yourself the opportunities to allow those changes to take place within the physical form. This way your form will be more conducive to facilitating access to greater light, to enlightenment and the means whereby you can become less dense and vibrate at a higher frequency.

You are here in this life to change your physical body into a spiritual body - you are to become Christ-conscious beings. In the past, the feminine energy [Eve tempted by the Serpent - the Lucifer Spirits] led humanity into matter. Now it will lead you out again into the light and love of All-That-Is.

Fuel for the body

Realise that more than ever before, because of your desire to go home, an acceleration is taking place. Your bodies will need to be in harmony with your desire. The fuel you give your body needs to be attended to with great care. On the shelves of your supermarkets, and in the fruit and vegetable shops, are many poisons. There are toxins and we would even go so far as to say that even the additives that appear to be healthy are not necessarily natural and healthy to the body. If they are synthetically produced they will cause destruction of certain biochemical pathways in your body system.

Your body system, as soon as it comes face to face with synthetic chemicals of any description, creates a crisis and causes trauma within your body which will lessen your life and create for you a separation away from the direction in which you are choosing to travel. Your body will be negatively affected when you take chemicals or anything else that is foreign and not of this Earth in a naturally created form. Many of you who are experiencing allergic responses will find that you are reacting to the chemicals in the foods and not so much to the food itself. We encourage you to be very careful, very aware of the foods you eat. Let them always be of the highest frequencies, that of the living plant. A decision was made even before you were born, at the time of the Garden of Eden, that the plants of this Earth would allow to be assimilated into your system. The agreement was made so that the life-force in the plant would become the Life force expressed through the human consciousness. In a similar way, the plant kingdom had an agreement with the mineral kingdom. The minerals would be assimilated into the plant so that you would assimilate the mineral kingdom through the plant into your own system. You are full of minerals. You have zinc and copper, lead and silica and many other minerals in your system. You are a little bit of your planet! There is the same proportion in your planet as in your body. When that proportion is out of balance your body will not be able to function in the way that is appropriate for it. Your planet is in many ways not able to give you the correct proportions of what is required by you because the Earth itself is lacking and for many reasons the soil has been leached of minerals. Many of the minerals have been locked up in the polar ice caps and you are unable to access them. Your pharmacologists are creating supplements that are synthetic in nature. These are not acceptable to the body and can not be integrated. Do your research. Find out what is required by the body so your body may function in harmony.

Initially, those of you who are not growing vegetables and herbs and various others required by your body, can walk around the supermarket and *attune* to the supermarket shelves. "Oh my goodness, I cannot buy that tin. I cannot buy that jar. I have to buy..." There is a particular piece of silverbeet that is calling out: "Come over here, I want to go home with you" and there is a tomato smiling and winking at you: "Take me home - I am good for you."

Be in harmony with those energies and you will find that as you walk around with your thymus gland open, your thymus gland will be the messenger as to what you need right now. This week you may need pumpkin. Next week you may need cabbage and the week after, silverbeet. Yes, you may need all three in one sitting! It is for you to determine, to *feel* and *sense*. Be in harmony with the food you take into your body.

During this period of time when the Earth is moving through the transition, take the natural supplements required by your body. Your immune systems are going to be subject to onslaughts in the very near future, so we encourage you to take the necessary precautions. There will be a shifting and changing and a releasing of certain toxic forces that have been locked up for a period of time. It is for you to provide what is required, for you to sustain and strengthen your physical bodies so they do not threaten your health.

There was a time in the far distant past when there was nothing remotely like a human being walking on this planet. There were angels and archangels. They did not need food the way you do. They ate of the pure vibration of the etheric substances. They had no physical form and therefore no need to partake of the physical planet and they would not have been able to, because there was no physical planet. The lowest expression of form was simply of the etheric forms.

A time is approaching when you too will be able to live simply off the etheric substances and you are beginning that educational process. That is why many of you feel the need to have only vegetables and fruit, for it is the closest you have to the etheric vibration. Experience how it vitalises *you*, thus will you facilitate that transformational process. Your bodies will then be able to vibrate at that higher frequency and you will become harmonised with the mind and the emotions, to become as one in the spiritualising process.

Question: In the Bible it says: "Two will be in a field, one will be taken up and one will be left". I listened to a tape from St. Germain and he said: "There will be two of you together and all of a sudden, one will be gone". I got the impression, that person would be lifted up and away from this dimension.

In the example given in your Bible the field does not necessarily represent two people working at tilling the soil. The field is the planet, the Earth upon which you live. As the Earth begins its separation from a third-dimensional world into a multi-dimensional world, the person who most resonates to the third dimension will remain with that world and the one who harmonises with the higher dimensions will remain connected to the evolving transformational or ascending world. Many of you already find that people who do not resonate with you are disappearing from your life. Even family members who have nothing in common are no longer maintaining relationships.

Cosmic energies

The energies being poured upon the planet, the cosmic rays, electrical and magnetic, cosmic in their derivation of variety, are given to assist you. They are the very energies that will assist you to move through this transformation with ease.

There are many kinds of cosmic rays. Some of them are electrical and some magnetic. These flow into the very planet, and because of their nature create a variety of traumas all over the world. While some of these are detrimental to humanity, at the same time, there are other forces at work to remind you of the patterns that are taking shape in the inner brain.

Crop circles

For example, the crop circles that manifest year after year on your planet are one example of the expression of electromagnetic energies. Patterns are formed along those energy grid lines. The areas along these grid lines are being used as a planetary artists' canvas because of the uniqueness of their etheric energy and the ease of imprinting an image. The dimensional layers are not quite so dense. They respond in similar ways to the akashic records and are used by many beings from different dimensions. Some are master teachers from earlier cycles, others are extraterrestrial. Each is sending its message to humanity through this medium of communication. Each being has its own particular signature.

In a way, your planet is like one huge brain. The lines of force create multi-dimensional patterns that flow throughout your world. There are more prominent lines that flow from England through

Egypt, from Egypt through India, through South America, moving through various patterns and linking up in various interlocking spiral lines of force that some may call the Dragon Lines. These Dragon Lines have focal points which pull the energy into them. They facilitate the changes in the very planet. These are the positive influences.

Let us return to the personal level. The new energies pouring into the Earth are necessary to assist in your own individual transformation and physical regeneration. If you do not utilise the energies for personal change, they are deflected and accumulate in the various stratas of the planet. For example, anger or unresolved conflict that has been stored as hostile rage over long periods in the individual, community, or country, needs to be expressed and resolved in an appropriate way. When you use the new cosmic energies to assist you in healing your personal anger, or any similar emotion, you will prevent the energy from being deflected into the planet or atmosphere. If *not* utilised, it will contribute to atmospheric changes, ultimately creating storms, cyclones and floods that unleash the hostility and rage upon the peoples.

There is a very important spiritual principle that is to be understood by all in this time of transformation. What is denied or repressed within the individual or group will display itself in an external way. When group action is required to facilitate change, but the group refuses to act on necessary social, political, educational or health issues, then the energy that has been available for that action is translated on the physical plane as earthquakes, storms and the like.

Consciously creating the future

The cosmic rays flowing into your planet are facilitating the changes in the DNA, the very genetic coding, to enable an awakening of skills and abilities which have been lying dormant for so very long. The frontal portion of your brain responds to the images you hold and activating the image will create new pathways in the brain.

Each of you is now being compelled to use your mind, to use your brain, and to use the faculty of imagination in a very specific way. We do not need to state to you that you are being requested to change. You are being compelled to change. Everything around you is compelling change, change, change! The willingness of you as an individual to facilitate change will determine the way that change occurs. Many of you resist the changes. Many of you resist looking to your future, resist making decisions. You refuse to communicate your desires to express your passions and your compassions, closing the door on what is potential and preferring to hold on to what you have.

We will explain. If you were to step under a shower with an open umbrella, you would not have a shower. The water would cascade either side of you and go down the drain, and ultimately end up being wasted according to its true purpose to cleanse the body. You, many of you, have an umbrella up, metaphorically speaking. The electro-magnetic waves that are entering your planet are not integrated and used, in the ways for which they are intended. These energies, instead of going into your body and into your brain to facilitate your brain to be activated, pour out instead as if you had an umbrella over your heads.

Brain, DNA and genetics

The genetic coding is a blueprint that was preprogrammed when humanity was very primitive and it is going through its evolutionary development in the same way a foetus develops into an adult. The evolutionary programs incorporated in the DNA are enabling certain genetic patterns to emerge to allow your physical body to undergo appropriate changes. Certain mutations are taking place to allow your physical bodies to go through the transition from a third-dimensional physical being into a multi-dimensional spiritual being. The DNA will enable the cellular structures to function differently. You will find a greater demand of your bodies to eat only the highest quality food in lesser amounts. You will become more discerning. You will find your body cannot accommodate what you have put into it before, and if you persist, you will surely become ill.

The neurotransmitters in your brain are now being activated and are being released to respond in new ways. These neurotransmitters have specific messages that advise the brain and your central nervous system how to initiate the changes in your body that will be in harmony with the transformations you are to be going through in the future. Gradually you are being attuned on all levels.

Chapter III
It Is Time To Go Home

CHAPTER THREE

It is Time To Go Home

A world in transition

We wish to share with you some of the patterns which we are formulating for you, and we will use the example of the sacrifice, resurrection and ascension of the one you know as the Son of God.

He has been known by many names. You have also known him as Jesus, the Chosen One, that Being of light, who was with you from the very beginning of Earth's expression and had a number of incarnations, yet always with a specific purpose. The light that was in Jesus has been present throughout all ages of time at the changing of times and the preparing of the way.

We speak now of the period of time when this Being of light was upon the cross. During that time there was a piercing of the flesh, and the releasing of body fluids which flowed into the very Earth itself. The physical flowing of the essence of that Man of God into the Earth had a significant effect upon the planet. Have you ever thought of the significance of that event? We would ask you to think for a moment of that event. It was a physical demonstration of the spiritual forces entering into and impregnating the very Earth itself. Understand the significance of that - the very Earth, the tangible substance upon which you walk, was spiritualised by the linking, the cojoining of the blood that had been spiritualised by the Christ principle. The blood of Christ blended with the Earth at that time to enable the spiritualising of the physical plane. That event in history laid the foundations and began the process of activating and awakening the spiritualising of matter. From that time onwards, the whole Earth changed. The energy, that was indeed the auric field of the Christ Spirit, flowed into the Earth and into the atmosphere around the Earth, so that you can say each of you has your dwelling place within the Christ light.

The transformation of the Earth and humanity has taken the 2000 years since. Every living thing has incorporated that spiritual essence into itself on the cellular level. That essence is incorporated in the food you eat, the water you drink and the total expression of nature.

Two purposes were served. It enabled the light of the Christ to flow into matter. That deepening provided the opportunity for the human soul, the spiritual being that you are, to have access to that higher light source, yet move into the depths of matter. During the last 2000 years, you have extended yourself even further into learning how to master the material plane. Secondly, that event established a blueprint to provide you with the clues to find your way home.

You may look back over the last several hundred years and realise that there have been great advances in sciences and technologies. These have happened for a variety of reasons and with a variety of influences, too complex for us to explain at this particular stage. We mention them to plant the seed.

As spiritual Beings, you needed to have the impulse from that particular period of time 2000 years ago to begin the awakening process. It was the drawing out from the unconscious into the subconscious, and now into the conscious, and with consciousness now you have gone deeply into all the dimensions of matter. You have burned your fingers financially, some of you. You are suffering in other areas of your life where there has not been the fulfilment which you desire. You have watched what you consider the degradation of your world, yet with that, there has been the anchor that has linked you to the stars.

There are those of you who are in a hurry to go back to the stars. You want to go home. May we suggest you will not learn anywhere near as fast up there as you do down here! Do not be in a hurry. You are here to spiritualise your physical plane. You are in the process of awakening to the awareness that you have taken yourselves as far as possible into the extremities of matter and now it is time to go home. Your physical bodies are quivering with excitement, yes? You feel as if there are many earthquakes occurring in your body, is that not so?

During the period of time when the masters, the disciples and the great beings walked with the Son of God, you were amongst those people. Yes, you were all there!! You did not decide to look over the edge of the cloud and just have a peep and say "Aren't they having a miserable time" or "Aren't they having a wonderful time". You were there! All of you have chosen to be there at crucial periods of time in the transformation of your world.

Another 2000 years have passed and you are here again. The Son of God walks amongst you in a different guise. This time the Spirit will not come as a physical representation flowing from the physical body of a man on a cross to flow into the Earth, to activate the Earth. It will not happen that way again! Do you understand? This time it will happen in a different way.

The Aquarian Age is the age where each person will become a Christed being. The water bearer pours down upon you the spiritual forces to enable each to awaken and embrace his own Christ within. Each of you will become Christ conscious. Each will move through his or her own resurrection and ascension in full consciousness, as was demonstrated by Jesus.

The spiritual forces will indeed *flow*. They will pour down and activate the etheric field, the vital force field that is in the hearts and souls of every one of you, that touches the very cells on the next dimension and will in that same process activate the Earth on the etheric level. The rumblings you feel are the shifting and changing.

You have heard about grid systems. They flow through England and America, from Hawaii to Egypt, from New Zealand to Hawaii and Ayers Rock, *everywhere*! It is a wonderful, powerful grid system, and you have the same grid systems in your body, the etheric channels through which the energy is flowing. This is what is being activated now. This is the preparation stage. This is the build up that is taking place for all of you!

Each of you is being prepared for the transition. Your internal energy system is gradually being strengthened to enable the greater spiritual forces to move through you without burning you. Remember the principle of the Holy Spirit. It is a fire that purifies and cleanses. It flows through the meridians in your body. It is sometimes known as the power of kundalini. When it reaches the crown chakra on its journey from the base of your spine, and after you have been cleansed of all of your fears and blockages, it then enables each of you to perform miracles as Jesus demonstrated.

Moving through the vortex

Your Mother, your Earth, she has called you forth to be with her as you each give birth to yourself. She reminds you that you have walked upon her breasts, you have walked upon her belly, you have walked amongst her valleys, her ridges, her mountains. You have swum in her streams. You have enriched yourselves. You have come forth again and again, lifetime after lifetime. You have given birth to yourself. She is the flesh of which you are made. She has come to tell you that she is transforming her flesh into Spirit, your flesh into Spirit. She will be ushered through the vortex of Life by those Mighty Ones who are gathered at the gateway between time and space, to carry you with your Mother, *into a place to which you have never been before, into a place where there will be two suns in your heavens, into a place where the stars in the sky will be of a different configuration.*

You will be carried, ushered through, held by those who love you. It will be as if your Mother, the Earth upon which you walk is being held in the arms of the Mighty Ones as they carry you forth into that experience, into that Life that has not been lived before. Your bodies will be changed. They will not be bodies like you have now. They will be likened unto the Spirit from whence they came; form, yet not form as you know form to be. They will be shining forth a light that sings its own song, a tune that is in greater harmony with the harmony of the sound of your universe, bringing forth the colours that are more in harmony with the true colours of the Universe.

As we see you, we see around you a colour field that is broad and wide and high and deep. We see not your eyes as you see your eyes, nor your face as you see your face. We see not arms or legs or body, we see colour and we hear sound. We *know* you by the colours which surround you. When we see your colours we know you as we have known you before. Yet the colours we see have been dulled through the times you have allowed yourself to bind to a resonance that restricts the fuller expression of that which you truly are. Now there is pouring down upon your planet, and upon the very flesh of your bones, a vibration that will assist you to bring about that change, so we will see you in a different light, as a different light, in a colour that vibrates in beauty, in harmony and in balance. When we are able to see those colours, we will know that it is the time that we may lift you and usher you through that vortex.

When you emerge into that place and look to the stars you will know that you have come through, for the suns will shine in a way that you will shed new light on yourselves. You have heard of the seven rays? You have heard of the nine rays, you have heard of the twelve. You will vibrate to all of those rays, and each of those rays will create the most beautiful pattern. You have heard of the very structure of your DNA forming the double helix. It is a wonderful spiral that moves in patterns so precisely to create the very foundation of your body. You will harmonise with this spiral as you move through the very galaxy in harmony with a greater spiral, weaving and blending - the microcosm in the macrocosm.

Mother Earth (Hakawaya, a Shoshone Shaman Indian speaks)

Your Mother awaits you. Your Mother embraces you. She has nourished you with the milk of the land. She has given of herself without withholding. With all her love she has been willing to allow you to tear her apart, to poison her body, to denigrate her, and she loves you yet. Children, children, when will you cease? When will

51

you love your Mother? For in this time that is approaching, she will rumble and she will shake, and she will cast aside those who do not honour her. For her it is the time now to call to herself those who love her, to embrace those who serve. She knows those who are her children. Honour your ancestors, she tells you. Those who have gone before you have laid the foundations of all time. Read the signs, for as the wind blows, as the water ripples from mountain tops to valleys, as the sun shines upon the parched earth, she speaks to you. Her message: Tend your children, tend your Mother, tend and embrace all of nature.

All of you here have been Red man or Red woman before. You have sat at the door of the teepee. You have sung the songs and danced the dance. All was told to you before you came to this body. You were told that this life and this land would reveal themselves to you. It is required by you to right the wrongs of the past and to be willing to enrich the soil, to cleanse the rivers, to bring fragrance again to the air, to walk in peace with brother and sister, to ride the wild buffalo across the plains - then will you understand the relationship between all life.

You have lost your roots. You have forgotten who you are. You no longer talk to the air. You no longer understand what your Mother is telling you. You turn your back against the wind. You feel it not as your friend. The mountains, you have placed them too far away, too high to climb. Like the eagle you soared, for then when you were Red man, you climbed the mountains to the eagles, and you found the mountain lion and you found the owl of night. You understood the cry of the coyote, you reached out to the embrace of the whisper that contained the message to your soul.

Travel forth, you who will again reconnect to all life. Travel forth and become at one again with Nature. You cannot aspire to the heights unless you understand the Earth upon which you walk. In past times as you walked upon the Earth, your Mother, you listened as she spoke to you. Now you have forgotten how to hear her voice. Reconnect! She awaits you. She will carry you from her womb, and she will set you free. Hear the call.

Ishtar speaks

There is a rising in the shift of consciousness concerning the value of your planet. You will find this value increasing in the years ahead. You will become aware that your land is precious and will begin to treat it differently. In your relationship to the Earth, you will activate the spiritual soul, for in the love that you give to your planet, you will find equal return to your soul.

In discussing ways in which you can become more spiritual, we include developing a relationship to the very Earth upon which you walk. Develop a relationship with all living forms, plants, trees, and rocks, as well as extending yourself to the birds and the animals. Each in its own way becomes a reflection of God/Goddess/All-That-Is and, as you open up to creating a relationship with the living forms, you are extending and expanding your spirituality.

So we encourage you, even if you have only a flower pot in the bathroom or the kitchen, to create it as a shrine, as a sacred place. Those of you who have the benefit of a piece of land upon which your house is situated, develop that as a sacred site. Treat it with sacredness. Be willing to walk around without shoes and feel the essence of the energy flowing between you and the Earth, and between the Earth and you. Allow yourself to put your hands in the Earth, to touch the trees, to listen to the sounds of nature, to walk in the glory of all that is the expression of All-That-Is.

The more love, the more energy and vitality you are able to place into the sacred soil, the greater will be the stability of the land. Many who are not connected to their land, will experience upheavals. Find your connection with Earth, and talk to the Earth, and the Earth will talk to you. In the years to come, those who are open and have developed their spiritual senses will become attuned to higher frequencies. They will hear their guidance and follow the message. The future now is unfolding quite rapidly and your planet is establishing new lines of force, creating new intersections, as it were, within the planet itself. Upon these will be established the temples of light.

These temples will be quite vast in their impact and will become sanctuaries for the many. In these sanctuaries opportunities will be given to all those who have been the forerunners, to teach and heal those who follow behind. There will be a new level of communication such as you experienced of old. We speak of telepathy. There will also be a greater activation of abilities to see beyond the physical.

Thousands and thousands of these temples of light will spring up around the world. People will gravitate to them according to their own resonance, and there will be shiftings to and fro. You will find that it will take some time before each finds his natural path and some may go to one place and feel not quite at home, and others will gravitate to yet another and feel a little more at home. We are not saying every person is going to be in a temple of light, any more than we can say every person on your planet has to be working as you are working. How would it be if everyone was the same? You have created a world of diversity and you will discover more of that diversity in the years to come. Realise that the planet is also an evolving consciousness. It is by far more advanced than you in your consciousness. It *already* exists in its conscious awareness above and beyond anything you can conceive of as third dimension.

We have said to you that the light entering your brain is causing changes within it. That same light has entered into the Earth. We do not want you to be concerned about where the light is entering, only to know that it is entering through all the vortices of your planet.

As you look back, those of you who are inclined to look back, at a period of time approximately 12,800 years ago you may recall it was the final destruction of that land known as Atlantis. It was also the ending of the Ice Age. That period of time saw many changes taking place on your world. Those changes were the result of a powerful destructive cycle brought about by the misuse of power within the Atlantean culture. You are now moving into a period of time where the negative forces of that cycle are to be changed to positive forces and a period of total transformation and a reversal of those old patterns is to take place. It does not necessarily indicate that you will create for yourself another Ice Age. More specifically you will enable yourself to move beyond the limitations of your third-dimensional world so that you no longer need to be a victim of the forces of nature but rather learn to unite and befriend them.

Powerful forces and powerful energies are coming in, so that those of you who have made the decision 'now or never' are here in this particular place on Earth at this specific period of time in your Earth's history to participate in the greatest opportunity that has ever been available. You are *now* giving yourself the opportunity, because never before has it been quite the right time.

It will be progression. It will be activation and awakening. You will feel as if your conscious mind is expanding and as if you are living in several worlds at the same time. Some of you are catching a glimpse of that already. It will happen more and more. As you move symbolically through the gate that will take you into the sense of timelessness, you will feel more and more as if time is your friend. We suggest to those of you who feel as if everything is going so fast, there is more to do in less time. When you find yourself rushing hither and thither, know that is the time for you to stand still in the quietness and to find your centre. Know that you are moving away from an outwardly motivated expression to an internal focus. External action is the expression of masculine energy. It has served well in the desire to experience the material plane. That energy is part of every person whether male or female.

It is the masculine energy that takes you away from your Source in its desire to penetrate the farthest and the deepest. It is the feminine energy that calls you home. The feminine energy unites and binds together. Each of you, whether you are male or female, has both energies. Your male energy is very active. It keeps you busy in the 'doing' of life. Your feminine energy is passive. It enables you to 'be'. It asks you to be receptive, to listen, to wait expectantly for the inflow of the love and light of God/Goddess. Goddess is now calling you *home*. Your task is to listen and to respond. She will be represented in your relationship to your Earth home.

It is time to take notice of your Earth again and it is time to reunite with yourself again - time to be still, to be quiet, when your whole world seems to be in chaos. Stop. Be silent. Allow your inner Self to reunite again with its Source. In this way you will move into the greater dimension of awareness. During this period of time, the energy that has previously moved in one direction, will slow right down and will then begin to move in the opposite direction. This will have an impact on the ocean currents, wind direction and changing weather conditions. It will ultimately shift the balance of power from the northern hemisphere to the southern hemisphere.

Have you, as a child, used one of those spinning tops? You have seen the top spin round and around in one direction and you have watched it as it slows down. What happens, as it slows down, is that it begins to wobble. You are in the *wobble*! You are wobbling, and you will wobble a little bit longer. The *world* is wobbling. That is why there is much trauma, much tragedy in your world. You will experience this in an energetic way. What is required by all of you is to assist in the shifting of the energy flow so that the top - yes, your world - will start to move, etherically speaking, in a new way. Remember, we have talked about the physical body being activated. The etheric body is being activated now, and its spiral will be in the opposite direction.

So you have one energy going one way, and the other going in the opposite direction, and these need to move in harmony. When they move in harmony, the male and the female energy will move in such a manner that equilibrium will be reached. It will set in motion access to a new energy system - a higher level of electrical, magnetic energy that will be available to all who choose to use it.

Weather and Earth changes

Yes, there are volcanic eruptions and earthquakes, there are seasons that seem to be changing and weather that seems to be more and more damaging, dramatic and violent. Each of you, in your awareness of self, even if you are isolated in a community, even though you may be separated from television and radio, will sense and know that something is changing. It almost seems as if it is out of your control, as if you are poised, waiting on the edge, ready to step off into an unknown. Even if you were not to have that awareness of the outside world, it is happening around you. You will have weather like you have never experienced before. In the coming seasons the weather will be experienced in surges, in harmony with the peaks and troughs of the flowing of the electromagnetic energy pouring into your planet.

This inflow of cosmic and electromagnetic radiations is a gift! Oh yes, it does not feel like a gift at times, but these energies provide you with the means for transformation. You as an individual will experience it flowing into your bodies through the gateways called chakras, activating your physical bodies; into and through those meridians so they can activate the neuronal pathways, and release certain chemicals so your physical bodies can change.

Similarly, there are gateways in your planet through which those radiations pour. They are accumulating in certain areas and like all accumulators where energy is stored, there comes a time when, if the energy is not used, it creates an over-abundance that is experienced either as weather or as the movement of the tectonic plates.

That cosmic radiation, as it is experienced in your own body, if it is not utilised, will be felt as trauma to the physical bodies. It will be experienced as 'weather'. Weather in your body is emotional upheavals and emotional disturbances rising to the surface. "I thought I had dealt with that! Oh, I thought I had dealt with that so long ago! How did that anger come to the surface and so spontaneously? I thought I was okay about that situation and suddenly I am crying all over the place! What is happening to me? Why am I so unstable and out of control again?" It is because this huge amount of energy is moving through and flowing into the little crevices, the nooks and crannies of your body and into the organs that you have shielded in the past. This energy is breaking through the shield of protection into your liver, oh yes, where you store those emotions. You wonder why you suddenly have liver problems or why your back is hurting. It is because all the old hurts from childhood that you thought you had successfully buried have suddenly surfaced.

Your own weather and your own body will be experienced in the same way; a sudden upsurge, onslaught, that seems to be out of your control, but it is there to remind you of what still needs to be healed so you can use that energy in a very powerful and positive way in your own transformation.

We will return to the weather. In the ways in which you are changing, so too is your planet. The inflow of radiation and electro-magnetic energies is creating instability, creating fluctuations, and the rapid build up causes storms around your planet, storms that will come unexpectedly. If they *are* expected, they will be unexpected in their ferocity, in their intensity and in the way in which you will experience them. Yes, there will be some ordinary winds and yet there will be also those that are very intense. Be aware that your country of Australia is preparing itself for the greater beautifying, the greater regeneration, the greater rejuvenation. The earth, the soil, is bare of nutrients. For so many thousands of years, the mineral content of your soil has been depleted causing diseased plants and diminished growth. There will be opportunities for rejuvenation of the soil, and ways to regenerate it so that plants can again grow to greater heights than those you see in the forests of southern Western Australia.

In preparation for the remineralisation and revegetation, you will experience storms of some intensity over the next three to four years. There will be, all around your planet, a greater activation of earth-quakes. These will cause you to feel a little bit precarious and you say "Are we safe here, where we are?"

Yes, in Australia, you are basically very safe. It will be *the* safest of all of the places to be. Yet you will not be totally without earth-quakes in Australia. There will be instabilities and some areas that will make you aware there is instability in the tectonic plates, even in Western Australia.

We are not suggesting the earthquakes will be large, about 3 or 4 on the Richter scale. Yet they will be larger in the Pacific. There will be those, already experienced in 1996, which will continue throughout the year, continuing into 1997 and beyond, some reaching 7.2 to 7.4 levels. These will be experienced in such a manner that you will be aware that there is a shifting and changing in the very fabric of your planet in preparation for the releasing of the energies and the old patterns. It will awaken a planet that is in harmony with humanity, and awaken humanity to be in harmony with the planet. There will be more fire and other symbols of energetic balancing and releasing, whether they be earthquake or volcano, for the energy that is not utilised by you as a humanity will flow into your planet and your planet will be over abundantly supplied causing an upsurge that will need to escape through earthquake or volcano. Some volcanoes will threaten and release steam, but will *not* spill over this year (1996) to create major traumas as has happened in the past. This releasing will enable a balancing throughout your planet.

You may experience change as waves of energy right down to the physical form where the planet is shaken, or it may simply be on an energetic level. We hasten to tell you that you have the potential to allow the change to take place simply on an energetic level. As you assimilate that energy flow and *utilise* it - and we stress the word 'utilise' - you will not need to have the energy dissipating into the land where the land itself shakes you up in order to tell you "Get moving!" *You* move! *You* do the moving, so that the planet does not have to shift and shake to do the moving for you.

Question: How important is it that we get the best quality of water and food for the changes that are to come about in us?

As we perceive, there will be very few transitional periods, and with transitional periods, we mean major transitional periods. One of those transitional periods has the potential to change access to ground water supplies. They will then have the potential of contaminating certain sources of water supplies which seem readily available now. We advise you create for yourself facilities whereby water will be cleansed as much as possible. This will not need to be an immediate concern even though there will be changes taking place seasonally in Western Australia.

There are two major factors which will affect your water supply and its quality. Firstly, in specific areas large volumes of water will be contaminated and thus be unsuitable for consumption. This will be experienced in many countries of your world. In many places already the price of water is acknowledged to be of more value than gold.

Secondly, the changes in weather patterns will cause drought conditions in some areas and open up availability in others with inadequate catchment facilities. Another concern for the quality of water is its oxygen content and state of aliveness. Many drink dead water which does very little to regenerate or cleanse your body. There will be new discoveries implemented and a whole new industry created to enable you to have a good supply of live water.

There will be a transition period where food will also need to be monitored. There only needs to be one more crop failure on your planet before there will be major concern for food reserves. The reserves of food around your planet are becoming quite a concern for those who monitor such activities.

Your Chinese people are presently moving through a revolution. They are waking up to the joys of alcohol and they are realising that alcohol is something they would like to have as part of their lives. Alcohol uses considerable amount of grain, does it not? When you have so many millions of Chinese, many of whom are beginning to drink grain alcohol, very soon the reserves of grain will diminish even further. There are grave concerns for the resources of food, both the food of the land and the food of the ocean. You cannot rely on them to continue as you have in the past and it is now essential that there be set in place procedures to maintain the quality of food, both in the ocean and on the land. The potential is there. We say this to you, keeping in mind that your planet is ascending, yet the period of time between now and the ascension is critical, or one which needs to be monitored from both the tangible physical and the spiritual.

The world as a mirror

Realise your external world is simply the mirror, the reflector of that which is taking place within you. It reflects your beliefs. It reflects your attitudes, and principally it reflects the decisions you are making. Many have decided they do not wish to be involved or take any responsibility for the well-being of the planet or your people and so they continue with their own destructive patterns. Because you have created those belief systems and attitudes, you have created a world that mirrors destruction and human tragedy.

That is why we have suggested to you it is now time to put energy into your planet. It is now time to begin the process of spiritualising. It will facilitate the transformational process and then the initiation, to initiate that transition from one dimension to another.

Earth, air, water and fire

Each element - earth, air, water and fire - can be represented by a personal dynamic. The element of earth equates with action (earthquakes). A refusal to take action may contribute to creating earthquakes on a grand scale. Failure or unwillingness to think and come to positive and conscious conclusions or make decisions in harmony with new visions can lead to cyclones and tornados being unleashed.

The element of fire represents the spirit of transformation. Each has the choice whether to transcend the physical limitation through the fire of the spirit or be forced to change through the element of fire. The Aquarian Age with the influence of Uranus will activate many fires and electrical storms, either positive on an internal, personal basis, or destructive to the environment. Those who awaken and express their internal 'fire' will assist in alleviating destruction of the external.

Diseases and their message

There will be an influx of new diseases on your planet; some are here already. Some have already experienced such diseases as chronic fatigue syndrome, diseases of the lymphatic system, diseases of the heart and vascular system and diseases that link to the thymus gland, your immune system. No one here has not heard of the AIDS epidemic. It too is a disease of the immune system, of the thymus gland.

There are new strains of tuberculosis coming to your planet, for which there is no known cure; strains of hepatitis affecting the liver, for which there is no known cure; and various blood disorders which have not yet even been identified. Other such viruses will find their way into your country, released as it were, from the jungles that are no longer in existence because of massive destruction.

Take care of your body, because the immune system will be challenged. It is dependent on the health of the thymus gland, which is the gland of protection. It is the gland nearest the heart, the organ of love. When the thymus is traumatised it may be a result of self-hatred, self-denial, lack of self-love or devaluing self in relationship to others. Guilt and shame also contribute trauma to the thymus gland. Defensiveness or defencelessness are also feelings that weaken the thymus.

The challenge for you is to open your heart, to love yourself enough to value your true Self. You will need to release the guilt and shame, overcome the fear of love and intimacy and see in what way you are defending yourself. You will not be able to take the negative feelings about yourself with you in your journey home. Remember, you are transforming your whole self, physically, emotionally and mentally. What is necessary is for you to care enough about yourself to go about the business of improving your life, your body and your relationships with those who are close to you.

You are now being compelled to access your emotionality, to get in touch with your feelings, to let yourselves feel the excitement, to feel the inflow of the spiritual essence of what the higher emotions represent.

You as an individual are changing your planet. You as a collective consciousness are assisting your planet in its healing. In many places you will see drought or flood or disaster. These are but mirrors to tell you of what is required of you so that you may change on a collective basis.

The universe is a hologram

Within each and every cell of your body, there is ALL - physical, emotional, astral, etheric, mental, spiritual - through all and on every dimension. Each cell is an antenna for the entire Universe. It is a hologram.

The year 2000 will facilitate a major change. At that time there are a number of planetary systems which will line up. These are a vast power. A proportion of light will pour through those vortices and those planets that will line up will cause a major shift in consciousness on this planet. At the same time, it will cause certain structural changes of the planet. It is a preparation for a metamorphosis that will be taking place. And we say here a *preparation*, for it is in that sense an activation of the planet and in the activation of the planet, of human consciousness as well. It will take from that time approximately another ten, fifteen or twenty years for the final stage of the metamorphosis. When we say the 'final stage' we are not saying it will be finished at that time. We are saying it will emerge.

We ask you to imagine the butterfly emerging from the chrysalis. It spreads its wings. It waits for its wings to dry. It tests its equipment, so to speak. It checks its legs. It learns how to use this new form. It is a new process. At that time the learning will then be facilitated. The changing will continue. The total metamorphosis will not take place by the year 2000. It will be activated and the continuation will be from that time. Chaos always begins before a new order comes in and chaos will be experienced on your planet.

Chaos before harmony

You will feel and sense the tragedy, the terror, the trauma and the suffering that will be experienced by many millions. It is a precursor of what is to come. There will be millions of refugees on your planet. There will also be such tragic loss of life. We tell you this because we wish you to see there is a polarity taking place, a polarity that will be extreme in all of its perceptions. There will be extreme trauma and tragedy and the extreme of experiences of light and love. There will also be the extreme of those of you who find your lives working so beautifully and powerfully, who have made the decision to participate where you become the co-creator of a new world.

When you see the extremities, realise that one will become the backdrop of the other and feel the momentum that will be created out of the extremes of one and the other. We encourage each of you to honour the changes you are individually involved in. You are not separate from your planet. You are not separate from the rest of the people on your planet. You are part of a group consciousness in the same way you are in All-That-Is and All-That-Is is in you. You are able to connect with the pain, suffering and loss and feelings of being displaced and homeless of those multiple millions who are walking around your planet. It will be the incentive for you to awaken the desire to *come home*.

We ask you, in the visions you hold, in the light and the love that you embrace and bring into yourself, to send out that love, that light, that vision of a future and embrace those who are experiencing tragedy. For as you can experience their feelings, you may also allow them to experience what you experience. They are as connected to you as you are to them. Yet, they are not as aware of your experience as you are aware of their experience.

Now we bring you back to yourselves. In your own personal lives, in what you thought was a stable life, you may suddenly find you have become somewhat disillusioned with what you have been doing. It is as if you are rethinking what you would like to do, as if what you had in mind has suddenly changed! You may even be in that void state, the void where you are uncertain as to the direction of your next move.

Some of you may have been told you will go through a period of darkness, that you will go through a period of the void. But it will not necessarily be a darkness as of night when the sun is clouded over. It will be a darkness of a different kind, a void of a different kind. In the void, it is as if nothing moves. It is like a vacuum. There is nothing, absolutely nothing. Many of you will experience your own individual voids, your own individual periods of crisis or darkness. You will feel uncertain, for there is no movement. "It is as if I am paralysed and unable to take any steps at all, and no matter what I attempt to do, nothing works. Nothing happens." It is a time that some would call *the dark night of the soul*. Others would call it the void. It is a state of consciousness that many will experience and it will last as long as it is required for the individuals that you are.

So allow the flexibility so you may embrace the changes, knowing you can make those decisions... "Oh yes, I have decided I am not really happy in this particular job I am doing. I think I will change it. I just might take a job in a totally different direction." We suggest, yes, you will do that, and then you may find that in twelve months, suddenly even that job has served its purpose and you are ready for another change. Also note that some will experience, even amongst those who are close to you, a level of insanity manifesting in a variety of ways.

For some, it will simply be that they will be making strange choices, totally out of character, as if there is no logical reason for what they are doing. If you talk to them in a logical way and say: "Why are you doing this? It doesn't make sense", they are surprised. To them it seems to make sense. It is a level of insanity.

Others will manifest their insanity by literally losing touch with reality. Many will find they are psychically 'touched', as if they are receiving Divine guidance and someone has spoken to them and they become the second Messiah. Another form of insanity. Still others will literally become insane in the traditional sense of the word. These will be varying types of psychoses, some of which do not have textbook descriptions. You will not be able to say: "Well, this person is definitely schizophrenic, and this person is definitely manic depressive." You will not be able to label as easily as has been the case, for there will be different types of psychoses. They will come to the surface in those not able to adjust to the changes taking place in their personal lives.

Suicides will also be prevalent with those unable to cope with the wide variety of different demands made upon them. They will be looking for the way out, a 'quick transformation'. There will be unexpected accidents, some on a grand scale. Many such experiences will come to your attention in the times ahead because of the inflow of the electrical and magnetic energies, causing activations within the physical body, which will be experienced on a very personal level. These serve to enable those who are ready and desirous of participating in those changes to lift themselves to a level of awareness.

You will experience in your planet the breaking down, breaking down, breaking down, in order to build up, to build up and transform! In these transitional times there may be nightmares for many people. Many will experience trauma and calamity, for in the transitional stages there will be many who will choose not to take off their blindfolds and will remain in the dark of their own ignorance, unable to see beyond. And there are those who are the visionaries and the dreamers of the future. They will create for themselves a world in which they give support and encouragement to many, yet will not need the experience of the nightmare.

Embrace the change, claim your power

Each of you is expanding and developing exponentially, faster than you have ever considered possible for you. Yes, change, rapid change. When you find yourself 'thrust out of the nest', out of the security of your past, into the unknown of what to do now, where to go next, it is then for you to say "What are my skills? How can I build on those? How can I utilise the information that comes from beyond myself so I can find the way to be creative and productive, to awaken the greater love, wisdom and power?"

Without exception, all of you will find that you have a unique task to do. Your task. In the discovery of your task you will find you are participating with many others such as yourselves in this whole transformation. We wish to excite you! We wish to inspire you with the awareness that you have entered in this year into one of the most powerful, creative and productive periods of your life. Yet because so many still hold on to the past and resist change, events are created that appear to be quite tragic, and traumatic to the individual, the family, the group, the country and to the nation. These are purposeful. They are to facilitate the ushering in of this totally new, revolutionary change. We can only say that you will feel and sense right down to the cellular levels of your bodies those changes taking place within you. You will feel the urgency. At other times you will feel yourself putting on the brakes, because it is going so fast. Perhaps you will want to bury yourself under the pillow from time to time, hide under the bed, and hope it will all go away!

Honour those particular feelings - it is important. Go into solitude, into your stillness, into your own darkness. It is in the darkness that a new light is born. It is in the depths of despair at times that you discover the new. It is during these periods of time when you go back into your inner self, that you will realise the new direction and the new opportunities that are available to you. As you are willing to step forward into the new, then will you emerge, bringing with you a new light, a new vibrancy.

Question: How may we assist ourselves to remain stable during those periods?

First we recommend you begin each morning and end each day with a period of silence, a period of centring and a period of activation and cleansing of each of the chakras of your body. Fill them with light. Fill them with love. Know that your energy runs not only through your body, but beyond to encompass the whole of your electromagnetic energy or auric field. Also find ways of utilising the energy by way of sending healing, prayers and distant healing, to other parts of your planet.

Create for yourself a sacred place on the very Earth itself. This may be on a small portion, even if you have a very small garden. Make a circle and maintain the circle as your sacred circle. Stand in the circle facing east and draw the energy through you, channelling it down into the very planet itself. In this way you will create for yourself a sacred place. You may choose to plant flowers, herbs, or anything else in the sacred space. It can be as small or as large as you choose it to be. Then you may sit and meditate in your sacred space. Commune with the Earth and listen to her voice. This will be your way of nourishing the planet. It will be your way of allowing energy to flow into the planet in your particular area, safeguarding it from the possibility of earthquakes. Earthquakes can occur when you are not utilising the electromagnetic energies being poured into your planet.

Enter the solitude

Each person will experience the changes in a unique way so each will handle it in slightly different ways. You will more easily assimilate change if you spend periods of time in solitude and silence each day. You will be able to assimilate your own personal changes, to think and to determine what has been taking place in your personal lives. Maintain a diary in which you record your dreams and visions.

It is the greatest challenge for most of you to enter into solitude, for it is very much like loneliness. Most of you are afraid that there is no-one there to love you. Know you are loved - develop a greater sense of intimacy with yourself, for it means that you get to know yourself, that you are willing to trust yourself and your own guidance. Whenever change takes place you need to trust that you will make your own decisions and be able and willing in that decision-making to take those next steps along the path in full confidence.

We are *not* suggesting you store food in your cupboards, nor that you develop a stockpile of gold and silver. Nor do we advise that you place yourself in the mountains so you do not have to experience a tidal wave. We say you accomplish one of your greatest assets - the ability to create what you want, when you want it, when you want to become the Master creator. Then wherever it is that you live, you can say: "I love it so much that I am going to pour all this love into the area so that it will maintain itself and grow and be rich and it will not be the victim of an attack, a target."

From fear to love

Question: Are we the catalyst for the consciousness of love?

The catalyst is love. Can you ever doubt? Love will always be the catalyst. Love is all there is ultimately. *Love is all there is.* Yet love is most feared by the greatest number of people throughout your whole planet. Many would prefer war and battle, keep at arm's length, avoid, run away, hide, deny, suppress, refuse intimacy, sharing or caring, rather than love. With love there are no secrets. With love all things are known, all things are possible. With love you do not deny yourself anything. Love provides you with everything, easily. Those who lack, who are in pain, it is because they refuse love. *If you find your life is not happy, it is because you refuse love.*

Love provides all things to all people. With absolute and total love, you would never ever need to attend any institution of learning, for with love you have all wisdom. With absolute and total love you would have all the riches, all the wealth, and all the resources that you would ever require, for *love denies nothing.* Love refuses nothing. Love is All-There-Is. To the degree you allow yourself to be loved by yourself and others, to the degree you are willing to open your heart, by that degree you will allow everything to flow easily, and have access to all resources. Oh yes, love is the key - the only key. And what prevents that love? - the fear, the guilt and the shame.

Heal your heart, the vessel of life, where the gift of love is given you. Oh yes, open your hearts and all will be well. Remove the veils, take away the shield. Allow the light to shine. Bring in those who work with you in the higher levels, for even as you open up to the greater love, do you invite in those beings who are your spiritual family, who have their expression in the higher frequencies of vibration.

When you communicate amongst yourselves, do so with reverence and with joy, do so with happiness, for love is sharing and caring, love is honour and respect. Love is value of self and the other. Love binds and links together. Love enjoins, love harbours no resentment, but understands all things.

You as the individual are responsible for the tune you are playing. You are responsible for enabling yourselves to release what is causing you discord, lacking in harmony with the All-That-Is. This discord is caused by mixed thinking, in that you say one thing and believe another. You have certain types of thoughts, yet you say something different from what you are thinking. Many of you do that without even considering the impact it has on the physical body. You are creating dissonance within your bodies and organs.

Realise that you are to bring your thoughts and the words you speak into harmony. You are to bring the subconscious into harmony with the conscious. If you have subconscious agendas of wanting to be loved, but being afraid to receive love, then these are conflicting. You want to be loved, but when someone gets close enough to love you, you close the door and you pull yourself back. These are conflicting messages that cause your internal organs to react in specific ways. They do not know what to do. "Am I supposed to open up to love, or am I supposed to close to love?" We wish to encourage you from now onwards, *do* watch those conflicting messages you are putting out all the time. In the actions you are involved in, how is your physical expression taking place? Are you actually saying you want to be successful, you want to go out there and do these things, and yet when the opportunities present themselves, you hold back?

70

You wonder why your foot hurts. You wonder why the sciatic nerve is pinching, why your spine is becoming immobilised. Each of these is an indicator. Your body is giving you the message: "You are giving me the message to go forward and so I supply you with the energy to go forward. But you, out of your fear of the consequences of going forward, pull back. It is like driving a car with the accelerator and the brake on at the same time!" It creates friction in your bodies.

Question: I have a very elderly and sick mother, who is very nasty to me. I wonder if this is something from another incarnation?

We say most definitely, yes. It is time the pattern changed. Each facilitates the other. You facilitate her to continue in the way that she is. It is time that she understood that her manner of speaking hurts you, distresses you. When you are willing to let her know...

I am now.

In which case you set up for both of you a way in which, if she continues to speak like that, you will walk out of the room.

I have done that, but I am concerned that if she passes over and this is not reconciled, we will have to have another life.

Not necessarily with her. Many marry and you think that because you have married such a person who perhaps is violent and abusive, that if you do not get on and like that person, even though they continue to be violent and abusive, you have to meet them in another lifetime.

Your lesson is to learn to love yourself enough to no longer tolerate that someone would treat you like that, to empower yourself sufficiently so that you respect yourself enough to no longer feel that you need to have that type of experience in your life. If you are willing to reflect to the other person that their behaviour is no longer acceptable to you, you yourself have made the decision that you no longer wish to have that experience in your life. Having made that decision, you will set up for yourself a very different experience, one in which the people who come into your life will be those who speak kindly to you, those who treat you with respect, those who embrace you with love. If your partner, your mother, your father or your children do not change, it is *they* who will one day face themselves in a new experience, not necessarily *you*. You have been willing to see what you do not wish to experience.

Joy

We want to emphasise again and again that each day of your life you need to affirm "I am here to have joy. What would I like to do today that I enjoy doing?" Then ask yourself: "What am I indeed doing that I prefer *not* to do?" "Well, I don't want to go to work any more..." We are not saying to you to throw in your job and forget about your responsibilities. It is not quite as simple as that.

First of all, each of you has come into this life to find what you love most. You have come to be both creative and productive. If you are doing something that does not provide the expression of creativity and productivity and as a result you feel disillusioned and unfulfilled, you may need to reassess your ultimate purpose and destiny. Each of you in your own way will find that there is something you would like to do that would give you fun and pleasure. Enjoyment and pleasure are equated with the lumbar region of your back. Many of you will stiffen up and have certain constraints when there is no fun, no joy in your lives.

So there you are, locked in, and your back locks into the rigid stance of having to do. It is time to loosen up and to allow the joints to loosen, because you see, there is this wonderful spiritual energy. It is a delightful spiritual energy. It is like liquid light. When it pours through your body it will heal your body. When you give this liquid light the slightest colour, it will bathe your body and your joints, and healing will take place.

Give this particular liquid light the colour of pink. Bring it through the top of your head and allow it to flow through in the most glorious way. It is a gentle trickle, like a sparkling stream, through all of the little undulations in your brain, bathing your brain, then down - do not forget your ears - pouring inside your ears, then down your throat, *all* the way down, so that it goes through the whole of your body. Liquid light coloured with the most beautiful shade of pink - a rose pink - the colour of love.

Take the love into your bodies, and in that way you will open up your bodies to be the receivers of love. Many of you who feel you have to *earn* the right to live, hold within you the belief that says: "I am not a good person. I am not acceptable. There is something terrible that I have done in this lifetime, or a previous lifetime." So you carry within you a shame which somehow says that you have to earn the right to live your life! Open your heart and allow the liquid light to change the old beliefs and instead incorporate into yourself the gift of life. Accept that gift as a gift from God/Goddess/All-That-Is.

It is time now to let go of the past, to heal yourself of any idea of guilt or shame; time to let go and be willing to allow the good things to come to you. For in that, you will find love is the key. Love IS the key. Many of you here do not love yourselves. We see it in your energy fields. You are moving toward the period of time when the God/Goddess will stand before you. She may hold a chalice overflowing with a liquid that bubbles like champagne and say to you, "Here you are!", and you may say "No, thank you very much. I haven't worked hard enough yet, I don't deserve it. I don't think so, thank you. It's okay that I do it for you, but not for me. I was such a rotten person in that other lifetime. Oh, yes I was! I let them down. In fact, I was so bad that I don't ever believe I deserve to be forgiven and I will hold on to that and turn my back so that I cannot ever receive anything, and I will always remain poverty stricken, whether it is in material terms or in my soul. I will never allow myself to have that relationship because it would mean someone could love me and I don't believe anyone would ever love me, so I don't have a relationship." Whatever it is, you have your own particular way of denying yourself because you have said any one of those things and we wish to remind you that, as you open up to being willing to be loved and being willing to love yourself, your life will change and you will bring to yourself the relationship that does seem to be so elusive, or that money that seems to escape through your fingers just when you have enough to buy yourself that special gift.

Whatever it is that you want to complete your life, the reason you do not have it is because of love. We will confirm that this is the time for dreaming dreams and to put in place what you would like to have for yourself and in doing so, ask yourself the question: "If I really wanted it and believed that I deserved it, why do I not have it now?"

Question: Could you explain to us why we are fearful of love?

There are four major reasons contributing to fear of love. The fear of being *betrayed, abandoned, humiliated or shamed, or imprisoned by love*. Each in its way will cause you to be fearful of embracing love. To overcome the fear each relationship will need to be treated as if it is brand new and does not have the overlay of previous relationships. To heal, change the old pattern that created the fear into a new and preferred pattern.

Chapter IV
The Grand Plan

CHAPTER FOUR

The Grand Plan

There is and always has been a Grand Plan decided upon by many who stepped into the holographic universe through specific gateways or vortices in order to experience. You are master creators and have given yourself the opportunity to create in as many varied ways as possible. Some of these creative endeavours have not always been of the highest integrity. In the process of your desire to create more and more opportunities to create more and more, you decided to explore the depth of matter, time, space and energy. You went through a series of 'falls' that took you down through the dimensional levels to experience and experiment, within this universe, the galactic and planetary sojourns that ultimately brought you to planet Earth. Some of the 'falls' were designed for specific purposes, others were brought about by conflict between the two forces that have been in existence since the beginning of your manifested universe.

These two forces, that of the feminine energy and that of the masculine, have played their way through all the cycles of downstepping. They may be perceived as the passive and the active. The interaction between them creates a third force and these three have been described as the Trinity in your holy Scriptures. The three principles of wisdom, love and power expressed in their diversity are the foundations upon which all of creation is built. When any of these is denied, suppressed or negatively expressed it has an impact on the creative process. The wars in heaven and on Earth are the result of the misuse of power, love and wisdom. In the beginning times, when the universe was young, these wars changed the very fabric of the universal matrix. Whole galaxies were created in new ways. Now your universe has stabilised itself into its own harmony of creation. The basic archetypes from which the universe has been created need to be maintained in balance. Chaos always seeks order and organisation.

The war in heaven

There was a major event that occurred in your recent history. It has been known and recorded as the War in Heaven. It occurred in the Hyperborean Epoch before your present humanity had begun its creative cycle. A number of Angels rebelled against the Archangel Jesus and this resulted in the expulsion of the rebel Angels, under the leadership of Lucifer, to the planet Mars. The coming Aquarian Age will confirm much of what has been stated here. In this age there will be a blend of the scientific and the spiritual. The War in Heaven caused a change in the entire planetary rhythm within the solar system, shifting the polar axis of all of the planets.

This was a 'fall' of cosmic proportions which called for corrective measures on a comparable scale. It was Christ who took on the task to restore the Earth and all of the planets in the solar system to their original divine order. The conflict between spirit and matter and the desire to have power and control was the cause of the War in Heaven. This battle will continue throughout time until spirit completely overcomes. The feminine pole holds the power of love and imagination. These were rejected by the Luciferians and this contributed to their 'fall'. Lucifer and his followers, when they came to Earth, imparted the knowledge they had gained to a premature humanity and this resulted in their expulsion from the 'Garden of Eden'. [More on this later]. They lost consciousness of their original divine Source. The Lucifers were bringers of light (from the tree of knowledge), yet the light was an illusion tainted by the desire to explore matter. It took humanity further away from its Source and deeper into the limitations of space and time.

Jesus took upon himself the task of redeeming the 'fallen Angels'. He descended to planet Earth after Lucifer and his followers took up residence on Earth. It was He, with many others, who were the Beings from Venus who became Master teachers to set up the principles that would enable humanity and the fallen angels to find their way home.

The age-old struggle

The struggle that you as a humanity are attempting to overcome is an age old struggle between the two forces of fire, that of the fire of spirit and that of the fire of passion and desire. The human passion and desire leads to war and conflict, the qualities of Mars and the influence of the Lucifer spirit. In your world the call to battle and war represents the sublimation of the Spirit of the Fire of Christ, symbolised also as the lion. In the Aquarian age the lion will rise in the Sphinx as she reveals her secrets. The Sphinx is a feminine form and will reveal the power of the feminine principles. The Hosts of Leo will stream a light-force upon your planet to activate the heart or centre of love. Thus will end what has been thousands of years of tyranny upon your planet.

As has been written "The Lion and the Lamb will lie down together". Do understand there is much more hidden in that statement. The revelations will be made clear in the Age to come. The Lamb of God (heart) and the Lion of the principle of Fire (mind) will again blend and harmonise. When you understand the magic of the fire of heart and mind and their higher application, then you will have youth eternal having resurrected the body of humanity into the spirit body of Christ. It is in the understanding and application of these principles that ascension will be fully achieved.

They who have abused the same principles in your recent cycles will be the healers of that abuse and will thus again enable the lamb and lion to lie down together. The Lamb of God refers to those who came to the rescue of those who were trapped in form without the means whereby they would find their way home.

The journey continues

If we are to follow your path from the higher dimensions to your present third dimension, we would say that you had passed through many star systems on your way to planet Earth. Many would confine themselves by saying they have only come from one star system. We would rather say you have been an intergalactic traveller and visited many, yet there is always one you will call home. Home is that star system through which you initially entered into this universe.

When speaking of the purpose behind the Grand Plan for the Ascension, for the spiritual potential of humanity, there are Grand Plans within Grand Plans, so we will do an overview of what we perceive is most significant in your present life cycle and the evolutionary pattern of humanity.

Very briefly we will summarise by describing the following. At a period of time in your distant past a group of beings entered your planet and interfered with what had been set in place by the greater architects of your world. Humanity was at such an early stage of its development it could be classified as more animal than human. The evolution from the human/animal into the human took many millions of years. To assist the process of evolution, intervention was seen as a practical step. Before this could take place, however, the first of many interferences took place. The separation of the sexes, as described in your Bible in the story of Adam and Eve, had already occurred. As soon as reproduction through the sexual act became part of the human expression there was an immediate transgression when the human males had sex with animals and created a progeny of red-haired monsters. This was a sin of unequalled proportions and it was necessary to correct the deviation as soon as possible.

Another event occurred which also had a traumatic impact on early humanity. A group of giant beings also entered the Earth, bringing with them the desire to manipulate the early native form. Some refer to them as Draconians, Dragons or Serpents. The temptation of Eve by the Serpent led to a separation from the divine Source. This was one of many 'falls'. These beings were a reptilian race who sought to control through altering the genetic pattern by breeding with the early natives. They defiled the early human form and eventually became trapped in the material plane by the consequences of their actions. They created a race of giants, the remnants of which can still be seen in some of your people.

In the beginning, all was in harmony in the kingdoms of nature and humanity. Each of the various expressions, from the mineral, through to plant, animal and human, was in tune and in harmony with the other. They gave support to each other, for each relied upon the other in their mutual interaction. They understood their relationship with the source of their Beingness. This all changed when interference from alien beings from other systems created discord and disharmony between the expressions of mineral, plant, animal and human.

The initial race of humanity was defiled over long periods of time. Sexual deviations between animal and human, and human and extraterrestrial continued until a genetic influence was introduced that created sterility in all situations of cross-breeding between species. Cross-breeding had resulted in many deviant forms, some of which are the mythological remnants of half human and half animal, such as the centaur. Others were a sub-human degenerated race of which the orang-outang, gorilla and the chimpanzee are reminders. Others who were half god/extraterrestrial and human created a race of giants. The Australian Aborigines are the survivors of this period of time having escaped the submergence of the land which destroyed many others.

The defiling of the human race due to two different types of deviation made it necessary to correct the deformities. A group of beings called the Lhas, Lyrans, or Els were invited to come into the planet on the continent of Lemuria. They were a highly evolved humanoid group of beings from a system of evolution which had run its course in the far distant past. They had reached a very high stage of development on their chain of worlds. Karmically the Lhas needed to return to the arena of physical causes, as they had not yet fully learned the lessons of compassion. They took on the task of becoming the guides and teachers of the Lemurian race which had been defiled. The Lhas had to be born into the bodies of the race as it was at that time. Their purpose was to evolve the degraded human form into the physical body of the future humanity. They were also seeking a deeper understanding of the secrets of immortality and creative thought.

The Lhas conferred with the Sirians whose involvement in the evolution of humanity was of primary importance. The resonance from Sirius resulted in the primary chromosomal patterns of humanity emulating the entire expression of the Sirian system. For example, the shape and angle of movement of Sirius B around Sirius A is the same shape as the double helix in the chromosomal configuration. The Sirians and the Lyrans or Els set in place the basic blueprint that was the reflection of the greater universe. It included the principles of number, shape, form and design as in geometry; the principles of chemistry and biology; the principles of life; that of creation, generation, degeneration and regeneration; movement, sound, music and colour and all that is included within the electromagnetic spectrum. These principles were laid down and taught in the Mystery schools.

From the period between 240,000 and 90,000 years ago Earth was visited by many races from within the Milky Way galaxy and beyond it. Many galactic gipsies visited Earth which, together with evolving humanity, became a galactic composite, as each group brought with it something from its home planet. For example, the beings from Venus brought wheat and the honey bee.

In the latter stage of this period a group of beings from the Orion constellation visited Earth with the explicit intention of seeking to control the race of beings who were living there. The Orions were a genetic mixture who had previously been influenced by the Lyrans. The Orions entered into the planet with the desire to control. Genetic manipulation was used to change the DNA. *Fear was genetically introduced into the DNA* creating a race of beings who experienced extreme fear and separation, so great that it caused many to hide in underground caverns. The damage that was created in the human psyche, the human soul, was so vast that it created a total separation from any connection with All-That-Is. From that time on humanity has been at war with itself in its endeavour to overcome fear and to survive, to protect and feel safe.

Each person who still harbours the genetic pattern within his chromosomes, will be required to heal the fear by facing the very dynamic that was the original insurgence upon them. It is the task of humanity to change its genetic pattern to its original form. The fear created feelings of defencelessness and defensiveness and set in place the beginning stages of the immune system for your bodies. The need for protection became paramount. Survival and fear dominated those who had been interfered with. This changed the whole fabric of the planet and was the beginning of conflict, wars and battles. Even the animals, which had previously been at peace, suddenly became aggressive and wild. With fear came the need to protect and the struggle for survival. The planet was thrown into an ice age (a much earlier ice age than your most recent experience) and humanity fell deeper into matter.

Your purpose now as a humanity is to face and heal that fear. You will recall and remember who you were prior to the genetic interference in your distant past, and you will heal yourself. Your scientists are beginning to understand the power of image in changing DNA. It is through this powerful feminine quality you will each be able to change your own DNA and heal your own specific fear. The fear will then no longer be part of DNA. Fear will be gone forever.

Fear is the very specific factor that prevents the union with the Source. All will need to face their fear. *Each person will place himself in a situation that resembles his greatest and his darkest fear.* If there is the denial of the fear, the refusal to face it, then the fear will change to anxiety, then into terror (terrorist attacks) and finally, if not addressed, into dread. It will go to such levels that you will feel totally debilitated. Yet, as a humanity, you will cause yourself to face your darkest hour and in facing your darkest hour, you will ascend the highest. It is in the greatest of that darkness that you will provide the impact to catapult you into your transcendence.

In the past times, Mystery schools were set up in Lemuria in the crystal cities to provide the foundations to heal the damage that had been done to the human blueprint.

Beings from Venus

A group of highly evolved beings who had stepped down from the Sirian system under the leadership of the one known to you now as Jesus [he was not called by that name at that time] assumed the task of being the redeemer of both the fallen angels and the defiled humanity. While the Lhas entered into the bodies of the early humanity, beings who came from Venus were under no such karmic responsibility. They were able to provide their own vehicles and they did not need to assume the physical limitations that were placed on the Lhas.

The beings from Venus were divine. They were a highly evolved race of beings who came to the planet to lay the principles for going 'home' again. They set up the temples of learning in the crystal cities high in the mountains. Their task was very specific and unique. They were to discover and set in place all that was required to enable humanity to find its way home. In the process, they were also to discover the principles of resurrection, immortality and ascension.

At the same time as the beings from Venus came to Earth as Master teachers, it was recognised that another very important step was needed. To protect the process that was set in place it was necessary to close the vortex through which so many were able to gain access. This was the vortex which is linked in a particular geometric configuration with the constellation of Sirius. Sirius provides the focal point through which this energy may spiral into your planet Earth. God/Goddess energy flows from beyond your universe through the Sirius vortex into the whole universe. When the vortex was sufficiently closed, to allow only a trickle of this energy to flow to sustain the feminine principle, it thrust Earth, the evolving humanity and all who were karmically linked, into the need to resolve and transform all of the dynamics that had created the 'fall' from grace.

When the Goddess vortex was closed 90,000 years ago you entered into a long period of learning how to apply the principles that were introduced by the Master teachers from Venus, sometimes called the Elder Beings.

As is the way of all karma, each individual or race repeats the old pattern until it realises its futility and decides to change. All of the beings who were in the grand play continue to participate. These include the Sirians, Pleiadians, Orions, Arcturans, Andromedans, Zetas, Draconians and many others from the galactic neighbourhood. Humanity is a mixture of many genetic influences.

Starseeds

Question: Can you please explain who the beings were who call themselves the Starseeds?

They were the beings seeded from the stars, sometimes called the Stellar Beings or Star Born. They had originated from other systems, both within your galaxy and also beyond it. They had achieved relatively high levels of advancement. They entered into your world during the times of Lemuria. They had for the most part been called to the crystal cities and been through that cycle of training which enabled them to reach a stage in their own spiritual development so that when the time came for Lemuria to be finished they decided to remain behind and assist a developing humanity. They held the memory of who they were, though buried deeply in their own inner selves. Throughout history they have travelled in waves, incarnating at specific times; at the changing of the ages or when humanity needed to be activated yet again. They carry the memory of their starry origins deep within their hearts. Theirs is always the mission to seek and find. They are the heroes and heroines, the leaders and the outspoken ones, who burned at the stake or died for a cause.

Many of you today who feel that you have your connection to the stars, belong to that group of beings who came in a wave to find the solutions and to create new spiritualised beings by changing the DNA from within, through the power of their own creative minds. It is now time for the Star People to wake up and recognise their mission. The way home is dependent on them.

Going home

As a humanity you have made the decision to go home. You have set in motion a series of events in your lives that has caused a quickening of time and a change in consciousness. As in the past you 'fell' from the higher dimension, now you are to return to those higher dimensions with conscious awareness.

In the past you created a body to enable you to express within the limitations of a third-dimensional world. Now you are creating a new body that will enable you to transcend the limitations of the same third-dimensional world. You are evolving a new body, a spiritual body. In order to do that you will need to evolve a new spirituality, not one that resembles the past, but something entirely new. You are evolving a new world and a new humanity. You are creating a spiritualised humanity. In order to do that you will need to change the genetic programs that have been in place for thousands of years.

Your world as you know it, is in the process of ending. It is crumbling right down to its very foundations. Everything in your world that belongs to an old way of expression - government, economics, education, arts, agriculture, science, health and religion - will go through its time of destruction. In the birthing of the Age of Aquarius will be found solutions of a different kind to the problems that belong to an age that has completed its time. The old ways of solving problems will no longer be appropriate.

In the times of which we have spoken you were downgraded into human/animal. Now you are to be upgraded into spiritualised human. You will not be saved by flying saucers or rescued from a world that appears to be in trauma. That is too much like the child who wants to escape from the responsibility of cleaning up its room. You have rather decided to take up the responsibility of finding the solutions so that you know how to do it. Then for all times you will know how to move consciously from one dimension into the multiplicity of all dimensions. You will have come of age as the true dreamers and visionaries, creating your own world.

Lemuria and the Lemurians

The Lemurians were beings who were very much connected to nature, to the Earth and the rhythms of the planet. They lived a cyclic life, having no concept of time as you know it now. Time as a controlling factor was not invented for many thousands of years. Time and space had very different meanings to your comprehension of it at this time.

In the early periods the Lemurians lived in large tribes and villages, using natural substances and fibres, building their houses out of straw and natural substances of the land. In the latter stages they used rocks and mud bricks and built cities that were quite advanced, though still in harmony with nature.

The Lemurians were taught skills in metallurgy, growing of food crops, craft, the making of pottery, animal husbandry, the mining of precious stones and the logging of forests. While they cut the trees and used them for building, this was done with great reverence and appreciation. They replanted as they logged and all was done so there was no destruction of the environment. They lived in total harmony with nature and acknowledged the great Goddess, the feminine energy. Their rituals and ceremony were in harmony with the cycles of the Moon and the solstices and equinoxes. They were telepathic and were also able to have conscious awareness of their relationship with the plants and the Earth itself. Their consciousness had a different quality than you have at this time. They shared a conscious empathy attuning to and knowing that which was the right thing to do. Part of the Great Plan for your future includes the re-emergence of the Lemurian consciousness.

The Lemurians also understood the elemental and magical relationship between ceremony and ritual and its impact on their everyday life. They celebrated the changing of seasons and the harvesting of their crops. They worshipped the Moon Gods and acknowledged those who were the 'gods' from the stars. They also recognized the great Goddess as the nourisher of nature. Lemuria may best be understood in her relationship with Goddess. It was only after the invasions of those who entered into the land that the love of Goddess was devalued. The remnants of the very early Lemurians may be found in the hunter gatherer tribes such as the Kalahari Bushmen or the Australian Aborigines. These were cut off from portions of Lemuria into more isolated regions after a major destructive period caused the break up of the larger Lemurian continent. This occurred between 80,000 to 90,000 years ago.

The indigenous people still hold on to many of the traditions established during early Lemurian times. Though long since contaminated by insurgences from Atlantean invasions at later times, many of the magical ceremonies lost their potency and full meaning of their original intent.

Mystery schools and crystal cities

Under the guidance of the teachers from Venus, the Mystery schools were set up high in the mountains in the crystal cities. Do not imagine they were of clear quartz crystals. They were partly made of many substances, some obsidian and alabaster and other substances that came out of the inner Earth at times of great volcanic up surgings. They shone with a brilliance that seemed to come from within. These were chosen because they maintained the purity of energy and because they held the consciousness and the resonance of the energy that was given to the people of that time. These crystal cities were built upon pillars of stone in the interior of the large island. There were no roads and no transport and it was impossible to climb to the top. Only those who were pure of heart were permitted into the crystal cities which were physically inaccessible and protected by their great height.

The Mystery schools set in the crystal cities were in harmony with the Seven Rays, each ray representing a specific path of destiny or purpose. Neophytes were chosen and called to the crystal cities and those who responded would find their way through the vast land of the interior to the centre where the huge stone pillars rose in columns into the air. The would-be students would travel for months, and sometimes years, to reach their destination.

Previously they would have had a dream and the dream would call them to the sacred cities. That they had recalled their dream and heard the message was an indication of their openness to be trained in the Mystery schools. That they were willing to follow the guidance and travel to their destination to the great interior showed that they were made of worthy material. They would find their way to the bottom of the huge pillars of stone and there they would have to find a way to ascend. Some would practise for weeks with little food or nourishment of any kind. They needed to change their body chemistry so as to become invisible, then teleport themselves up to the crystal cities. Before access was given to any place of sacred learning, each neophyte was tested thoroughly. The ability to enter the crystal cities was confirmation of the right to be there. Only those who were without fear, only those who were totally acting out of love and integrity were able to rise and be part of the crystal cities. They had no need of government, police or guard. There was no need for law enforcement agencies, for only those of pure heart and soul would be able to gain access.

The crystal cities were similar to your academic institutions of learning. Those who entered were taught for many, many years. Their whole lives were dedicated to gaining and understanding the principles of the universal spiritual laws. They learned and understood and were able to read the holographic images that connected all of humanity to their stellar origins and to their relationship with God/Goddess/All-That-Is. They became the healers, the dreamers, the teachers, the artisans, priests and prophets. They came to fulfil their own particular spiritual destiny. Those who were trained by the Dreamers were not only able to interpret dreams, they were also dreamers who dreamed dreams for others. You would perhaps say they were Master Creators for when they dreamed, the dream became real.

The teachers from Venus originated on Sirius and all Mystery schools throughout the planet that took the initiate beyond the third degree were based on the Sirian principles. Sirius holds the vibration of love and wisdom and all that is related to Goddess and her connection to Earth and nature worship. The great priest teachers throughout the ages such as Zadok, Melchizedek, Hermes, Merlin, Jesus, Zoroaster, Appolonius, Osiris, Akhnaton and many others, were teachers in the Mystery schools of Lemuria, who had come from Venus and Sirius.

Their ability to teleport in their physical bodies enabled them to go from village to village. They became the dreamers for the people in the village. They would walk amongst them and ask: "Do you have a dream that you wish to be dreamed?" and the people would come and say "Yes, I have a dream" and would talk about their dream. The dreamer would then dream with them, enter into their dream and enable it to become real, to become manifest.

Similarly, the healers had the ability to attune to where they were needed. They would appear in the village even before a disease would appear, even before people would find themselves to be ill. They were always there before the event, precognitive in their ability. As healers, they used the principles of spiritual law and for them the healing was instantaneous and miraculous for there was no need to delay the healing process. There was no need for healing to take time. Training in the Mystery schools continued over many thousands of years until there was a whole wave of beings who had achieved mastery. Earth was also going through its own changes and Lemuria was reaching its completion.

The Elder teachers recorded the information in huge crystals which were then taken to various places throughout the planet to be kept for a future generation. Included in this information was the history of the universe and all the events that had taken place to lay the foundations for the creation of the Earth, and all the kingdoms including humanity. The crystals also contained all steps necessary to enable you, as a future humanity, to ascend.

When the Lemurian cycle was complete, many of the Elder race and those who had completed their cycle on Earth, ascended as masters of that cycle, moving on to other dimensional expressions.

Others chose to remain behind and continue to participate in the journey on planet Earth. Some of the Elder teachers who chose to remain behind proceeded to establish Mystery schools in other places around the planet. These included the Andes in South America, the Yucatan, Mt. Shasta, Atlantis, Egypt, India, Tibet and Europe. Thoth, Merlin, Melchizedek, Abraham, Osiris and Isis were some who chose to remain behind to deposit the teachings in various places to maintain the secrets after the inundations.

Specially designed spacecraft were used to take the information to the various places around the planet. Many thousands of people were also taken to the areas where the teachings were to be established. Thousands and thousands of people were settled in the new areas. Many millions did not survive. They succumbed to the volcanic extruderances and fell victim to the floods and the fires. After the inundations that changed the land mass of Lemuria and the larger continent of Atlantis, the Mystery schools again came to life. The teachings continued to lay the foundations that would reveal the secrets of creation and the principles of transformation. The thread continued and still continues to the present time.

Question: Could you briefly describe the preparation through which we have been to enable us to ascend ?

As a wave of people, a wave of consciousness, you have been on this journey through vast numbers of galaxies, through vast periods of time, searching and seeking, exploring and experimenting. You were always discovering, with the whole purpose of mastery. We use the word mastery in a positive sense, not to have 'control over' but to master.

In the present cycle of time, you have experimented and practised in Lemuria and while there were those who ascended, who succeeded and rose above, they did not do it in the way in which you as a human consciousness will be doing. Certainly, they completed their cycle, but they did not go down into the depths of third dimension the way you have. You have also experienced and practised in Atlantis, again still not in the third dimension. You failed, due to those beings who would attempt to undermine and confound the desires of those who sought to transcend. Yet again, there was a dramatic failure, causing the planet and all the people therein to lose consciousness and memory of who they were.

So here you are now in the final stage, having in the previous 4000 to 5000 years awakened yourself again to that desire to go home. You have activated the flame and allowed yourself to remember your participation in the Mystery schools, whether in Lemuria, Atlantis, Egypt, Tibet, India or the Andes. It does not matter where. All who sense the flame burning in their hearts have studied in the Mystery schools throughout your planet. Now you will find your particular pathway to facilitate the awakening of your consciousness so you may overcome your own personal limitations; to find out what you individually as a consciousness will need to overcome in order to transcend the limitations of matter, energy, space and time.

You will find yourself in this lifetime doing what has never been done before. You are transforming your bodies and transforming your souls so you may reclaim your lost heritage, so you may return again to the Home that is your greater awareness of who you truly are as spiritual beings.

Chapter V
What Is The Aquarian Age

CHAPTER FIVE

What Is The Aquarian Age?

When you as a humanity first became physical, your spiritual Self needed to learn how to master matter. Step by step, epoch by epoch, you have stepped down into the deeper levels of physical expression. Having gone as far as you can, you are now poised to begin your journey home. The Aquarian Age provides the momentum to do just that. In the past, many have predicted the future and as is always possible when a child lives under the roof of the parent, the parent is able to tell the child what they can do. Then the child comes of age and decides it will do what it wants to do.

You are now coming of age. So when you ask: "What is to be in the Aquarian Age" we will say: "What do you wish? What do you wish to express in the Aquarian Age?"

It is not so much what is going to happen by way of prediction, as you are the ones who create your destiny. You are the Dreamers. When you learned to dream the dreams in Lemuria you learned that what you dreamed you could create, manifest. So now you are poised at the edge of a void and you must create a picture to step into.

The Aquarian Age is the age of the Dreamer. It is the age in which each and every person is able to express according to his particular desire, according to what allows him the greatest degree of joy and pleasure, the greatest degree of excitement! It is the age of the mind, not just the conscious mind, but the intuitive and the inspirational. It is the age of the creative mind and will take each and every person beyond the limitations of third-dimensional linear thinking into an expansion of thought so the Dreamer can again dream the dream and create.

Poised, you are looking at a world that is threatening to take you into your darkest hour and you are here now to realise that. As spiritualised human beings, your task and your challenge is to realise that your darkest hour is the compelling force to enable you to step into the Aquarian Age[1] with panache. You are to utilise what the Aquarian Age has to offer.

This Aquarian Age provides you with all the elements of the magician and the miracle maker so you may step out on to the stage with your magic wand, attune yourself to the spiritual forces and align yourself with your higher Self. Then, with all the beliefs, and trusting yourself and your abilities, you are to step forward into your future and determine what you want to create for it.

---

1 What creates an Aquarian age? (Author's note)

Precession of the Equinoxes

Hipparchus, a Greek astronomer who lived from approximately 180 BC, devised astronomical instruments to make star maps. He compiled a star catalogue and observed that the celestial pole moves by a few minutes of arc over a period of several years. This has been termed the precession of the Equinoxes. Earth processes into Aquarius every 26,000 years.

The Zodiac is divided into twelve sections of thirty degrees each. The sun on its annual journey travels through each of these in turn. The divisions are called the Houses or constellations of the Zodiac. Each house has a particular characteristic attributed to it according to the qualities and intensity of the sun's powers that are activated while it occupies the different parts of the Zodiac.

Animals are attributed to each of the signs. Each year the sun passes entirely around the Zodiac and returns to the point from which it started - the vernal equinox - and each year it falls just a little short of making the complete circle of the heavens in the allotted period of time. As a result, it crosses the equator just a little behind the spot in the zodiacal sign where it crossed the previous year. Each sign of the Zodiac consists of thirty degrees, and as the sun loses about one degree every seventy-two years, it regresses through one entire constellation (or sign) in approximately 2,160 years, and through the entire Zodiac in about 25,920 years. This retrograde motion is called the precession of the equinoxes. This means that in the course of about 25,920 years, which consists of one Great Solar or Platonic Year, each one of the twelve constellations occupies a position at the vernal equinox for nearly 2,160 years, and then gives way to the *previous* sign.

In the constellation of Taurus the Bull are also to be found 'The Seven Sisters', the Sacred Pleiades - famous to Freemasonry as the Seven Stars at the upper end of the Sacred Ladder. In ancient Egypt it was during this period when the vernal equinox was in the sign of Taurus that the Bull Apis was sacred to the Sun God, who was worshipped through the animal equivalent of the celestial song which he had impregnated with his presence at the time of its crossing in to the northern hemisphere. The ancient magical formula *abracadabra* refers to the bull. It means - The Bull, the only Bull; more correctly written Ab'r-achad-ab'r, i.e. Ab'r = the Bull, achad = the only etc. Serapis is also a name given to the Bull representing the only Sun in the heavens. It was during the Taurean Age that the associations between the Pleiades and the cow or bull became prominent. In many cultures where the cow is still worshipped there is a strong Pleiadian influence. Similarly the Age of Aries brought with it the worship of the lamb and the lamb became sacred as a sacrificial animal. The priests became shepherds of the people. In the Piscean Age was the fisher of men. He fed the multitudes with two small fish to demonstrate that he was a Sun God. In an earlier period we find the Goddess Isis with a fish on her head to demonstrate her association with Pisces. In the Zodiac, the sign opposite Pisces is Virgo, the Virgin or the Great Mother. Isis and Aphrodite also had their associations with Venus, the planet of love, beauty and harmony and the feminine principle. The custom of eating fish on Friday was to honour the great Goddess of Venus.

The Age of Aquarius is the Age of the Water Bearer. The Water Bearer is an androgynous angelic being who pours the water of eternal life on to humanity. In a personal sense the angelic being is our own higher Self or the Divinity within us. In this Age of Aquarius we may anticipate the downpouring of spiritual waters or a baptism of the Holy Spirit to assist us as we ascend into Christ Consciousness and eternal life. Each of us will become Christed. There is no need to wait for the second coming. We are the second coming. We are now going through our own initiations and preparing for resurrection and/or, ascension.

Movement of the Earth's axis

There are many ways in which you are preparing for the golden era on your planet, a time of peace and plenty. The symphony of movement of your planet around the sun is also co-ordinated with the greater plan and destiny of humanity.

Your Earth has an axis that is 23^0 off the vertical. Its movement around this axis creates your seasons, of which you describe four. Yet your world also wobbles around this axis in a similar way as you would see a top spinning and yet wobbling from side to side at the same time. You can imagine the axis of the top pointing in one direction and then gradually changing to point in the other direction.

A similar movement is also taking place with your Earth and this has quite an impact on the seasonal changes of your planet over long periods of time. It takes approximately 26,000 years for your Earth to complete a cyclic wobble on its axis. In the process, the axis will either point towards the sun or away from it. It is this particular event that is now contributing to your seasonal changes, along with the inflow of electromagnetic energies onto your planet.

The shift in the direction in which the axis is pointing is contributing to the heating of water in the oceans near the equator. This enables rain to fall over those regions which are at present major desert regions. As you move further into the Age of Aquarius you will find a change occurring that will enable your desert regions to once again become rich fertile regions as they were 13,000 years ago when the axis pointed in the same direction as it is moving toward at present.

There is ample evidence on your planet to indicate the presence of wild animals, such as tigers and lions, in regions that are now desert. Shells and fish fossils can also be found in the middle of deserts to indicate that in a previous time the area was covered with water. As recent as four to five thousand years ago the Egyptians hunted along the Nile valley covering an area where the Nile itself was far grander than it is at present. Many areas on your planet that you would classify as barren have already begun to feel the impact of the direction of change of the axis, including the desert regions of America, Australia and Africa. You may enjoy the anticipated benefits of these changes rather than interpret them as times of disaster.

What to expect

Question: Are we in the Age of Pisces moving into the Age of Aquarius? If so, how far away is it?

You are in both, for there is an overlap period. The Age of Aquarius has been with you since the inception of communication devices, your radios, telephones and televisions. Remember the time when your grandparents had their crystal radios. You may also recall the times of the first telephones, those strange contraptions with strange things that you attached to your ears. This was the beginning, the very first trickle if you will, of the Aquarian Age.

The Piscean Age has still not completely left. It will leave totally, completely in 1998 with only the remnant energies remaining after that period. There will still be those who attempt to hold on to an old age as did some who rebelled against Moses, the Monad for the Aryan Age. The rebels built the golden calf to affirm their desire to remain with the Age of Taurus. They eventually saw the error of their ways when they fell victim to the wrath of Moses. In a similar manner those who cling to the past will find it difficult to remain in a world that will move on regardless of their resistance to change.

From 1998, the greater impact of the Aquarian Age will begin to be felt. There will be major inventions that will be of the element of air, the element of communication and that which extends and expands consciousness into outer space. We are speaking of scientific inventions. There will be a worldwide focus on outer space and the greater desire for communication with extraterrestrials. Also you will see changes taking place in the areas of music, of the arts. There will be a great influx of beauty and of harmony, balancing those energies and forces that are to do with the soul. They will assist the soul to find its resonance and its family so that spirituality will emerge to be the union of soul and mind together as one.

This is the period of the expansion of the mind above and beyond what has been so far and the blending and unifying of beauty and harmony, so the soul will be nourished in harmony and bliss. For this is the balancing and the opportunity to bring together the appreciation of what is God and what is Goddess and how that is experienced within the spiritual human form.

This is the preparation of what is to be the accelerated Aquarian Dawning. You have been in the Aquarian Age of minor proportions for a considerable time, since the beginning of your communication. That will transcend whatever has been on your planet before! Communication, knowledge, information!

Communication a key

That is why in your personal lives you are being required to focus on communication. You prepared yourselves very well with the tongue. You have all that is required with vocal cords and epiglottis that sits quite comfortably in the back of your throat and various other internal organs that will assist with the mechanics of communication. Yet, many of you have not fully comprehended that beyond the physical communication, there are emotional and psychological blocks to communicating. What is another of your greatest fears on your planet, apart from loss of love and rejection and the myriad of others that align themselves with fear of loss of love?

Behind the fear of loss of love is the *fear of communication*, of speaking out, the fear of saying what is honestly on your mind, in your heart and in your soul. The Aquarian Age is the age of communication. Communication will be requested of you. And if we may, we will draw a parallel with the period of time when you did not have the need to communicate with words, the way you speak words now. There was a time in biblical history when a big tower, the Tower of Babel, was built. That tower ultimately caused a separation from God and a separation from the ability to communicate telepathically.

Previously there was but one language, the language of telepathy. It was a language where each and every one was able to attune, to know, to feel and to sense what was in the heart of another. There was no need for words. There was but one tongue, one word - the sacred word. Then came a myriad of words, a myriad of tongues and the need to learn the language which could be understood by the various cultures and races which developed. It was the beginning of separation and the development of individuation. You were there prior to the Tower of Babel, prior to the loss of abilities to communicate telepathically. Now you are fast moving towards the point where again, you are reaching the period of time where you regain what you lost.

We will use an analogy. In your communication devices you have what is called World Wide Internet. Communication is accessible to all, especially those who have a computer. Those who do not have the means to access do not know how to link into that technology. When there is an occurrence in the external world, there is an equal development taking place within the psyche or soul of the human. As you move into that realisation you will find the challenge will be communication, communication, communication. In the same way as you can connect to the Internet and communicate with anyone around the planet, you will also create pathways within your brain to enable telepathic communication to begin again as it was before.

To prepare for this you will each be required to heal your own fears around communication. It is time for each of you to address those previous life experiences when you were tortured, lost your tongue or were thrown in to the dungeons, either literally or metaphorically. It is time now for you to have the courage to speak out and be heard. It is time to speak your truth. Now we say this with certain reservations because we sense some of you may say: "Because I do not like that person I am working with, I think I will tell them." But of course they may say: "In that case you had better find another job!" While you have spoken your truth, it may not necessarily be the wise thing to say. When we say speak your truth, you speak it in the way that makes sense to your reason for staying in a job where you do not like your boss.

Imagine you have just found the job that is perfect for you in every way, except there is a flaw. There is a certain person in that job who somehow pricks you, causes you to be agitated, anxious or angry. In perceiving that particular person, it is for you in your honesty, in your willingness to communicate with yourself, to ask: "What do I need to learn from this particular person? What is it that I have within my soul, within my subconscious mind, that still needs to be healed, to be resolved?" As you do this, you would honestly be able to say: "Thank you for being a mirror for what is unresolved and not healed within me." You will find that every situation in which you find yourself, there is always a need for you to communicate with yourself to understand the dynamics you are involved in.

You are breaking through the veils between yourself and others, those barriers which prevent your openness. You will find in the acceleration taking place in the near future that what has been easily kept hidden, suppressed and denied, will no longer be that easy. You will find you need to face the situations, the dynamics, that have been a challenge for you. It is time now, because you see, not only are the veils dissolving around you and all of those with whom you have contact, the veils are also dissolving around your planet, and your planet is now opening itself to receive the downpour of multiple cosmic energies of a nature that will activate the very mechanisms within your brain, to assist the activation of a communication above and beyond what is known through the use of words. Information will again become freely available. The veils between the subconscious and unconscious levels are dissolving for it is in these levels that you store the memories of your personal past, of your planet, your past life experiences and even where those experiences and other planetary existences are inter-dimensionally stored. All are accessible.

The veils between these will begin to dissolve and each of you will find you will have easier access to the memory banks, which some may call the Akhashic records. So we do encourage you in your willingness to open to knowledge, open to wisdom, open to your multiple levels of the truth behind things, to realise that there is information available that exists from the past and also exists as potential futures for all of you.

Music and the arts

Musicians will create beautiful works of sound and quality that will far transcend anything that has ever been experienced before, a music that is in harmony with and aligns with the spiritual laws that will touch the soul, as the Psalmist David did. When playing his music he was able to change an emotion that appeased the king.

The artist will be able to create new designs, shape and form that align themselves with the human spirit. Do understand that the human form is created in accordance with a sacred geometry. It may be compared to the Holy Temple created at the time of Solomon. This temple was originally created in the Heavens to represent the incoming soul birthing itself from the heavens into the sacred womb. The artists of the Aquarian Age will be able to demonstrate their understanding of soul expressing itself in the vessel or chalice of the great feminine principle of Earth. When Earth is given its full value as the sacred feminine principle or vessel of the Cosmic Spirit, and embraced by the artist, the theologian and the scientist alike, then the Aquarian Age will have served its purpose.

As the scientists look around, they will see what can be done to create the ways, means and inspiration to express a knowledge that goes far deeper than what has been science of recent times. So you will find engineering, science, mathematics, physics, the medical fields and the arts all utilising an expansion of mind to draw on what is beyond the ordinary and the mundane, to create that which is new and innovative, to create a new world that will be heaven on Earth.

You will discover a vast new technology. You will find solutions to the problems that have begun to raise their ugly heads and demand attention. These problems range from the pollution of your oceans and rivers, a toxic chemical and nuclear waste that threatens the life of all humanity, diseases for which there appears to be no cure, depletion of the ozone layer, global warming, a reversal of the magnetic poles, a possible ice age and economic disaster. Many of these problems will escalate and appear to be insurmountable, yet with the innovative forces of an Aquarian Age you will be catapulted forward into realms of the mind that will astound you. These realms will provide you with many solutions.

New buildings

At present you have structures made out of substances that are solid, inflexible, thick and unwieldy. You will create new substances made of materials that your science has not yet discovered how to bind together. For example, there will be a fabric, a type of material that will be less than half a centimetre thick, but will be flexible and as strong as steel. You will build your homes with it. You will be able to see out of it and yet it will withstand the strongest of all pressures. It will be made of natural elements.

You will find yourselves living in homes that are so vastly different from what you have now. You will create motor vehicles that do not use rubber for tyres, metals for the frame or engines as you know them now. They will be entirely different and will move by virtue of the conscious interaction with the substance from which they are created. Your scientists are already experimenting with such things, already sensing the potential in their minds. We are speaking here of approximately 200 to 300 years in the future, but it is to be remembered that the Aquarian Age is over 2000 years in duration.

Technology - health

In the medical field, organs will be created out of similar things that look like the living flesh itself. Already they have created living flesh that is able to be put into the body when there have been burns or other such damage. There will be major scientific discoveries to change the genetic patterns so the body will create and repair itself, activating the reptilian brain which *knows* it can repair itself.

Solutions to a world in crisis

This world will provide the foundations for the solutions to the solutionless problems - overcoming the limitations of a material world, of gravity, space and time.

In the Aquarian Age you will discover much that will enable you to be free from what has been so soul-destroying, so threatening, so limiting and so disempowering. You will understand that nature is your friend and that all of life is indeed interconnected. You will see that nature is a living force and as individuals, when you work with this awareness, you will realise that each and every part of you is also connected to and able to communicate with all of nature. When you study nature with your heart and soul she will reveal her secrets. Within nature are the answers to many of your crises.

Technology of the mind

The lesson of life, in this present life, is to understand that you are a powerful technology within yourself, within your mind. You have the ability to create everything you want out of the very essence of what is available to you. It is not a matter of whether you have permission to do that. It is not that you need to ask whether or not you can have, or even that you have to work so very hard to create. It is rather the belief that you can have whatever you want.

It is not a crime, nor an adversity against nature or God, to live in fine houses and wear fine clothes. It is only that you believe that you should not have, or that you do not deserve. Even the gods, the extraterrestrials, lived in fine houses and wore fine clothes!

The raiment you will wear as you ascend to the high levels will shine like gossamer. It will glow like gold. It will have within it the essence and vibration of light and wisdom that provides all that is necessary. Those who own their physical bodies in their light form have indeed created beautiful homes and surrounded themselves with all that is an expression of beauty, all that expresses light and love. The individual person is to become self-empowered and is to overcome any idea that he or she is controlled by those external to them. These influences are but the remnants holding the genetic patterns of those beings who came so very long ago to your planet and who sought to control and intimidate through fear and to create the idea of loss of control. It is important now that each individual person be willing to overcome that limitation and reclaim the essence of his spirituality and his divinity.

As we have said, the Age of Aquarius is the age of the mind. At present you are using many different devices to communicate. You are using telephones, computers and televisions. At the same time, there is an expansion into greater levels of awareness and development of the higher organs of perception and communication.

Telepathic and clairaudient communication is becoming more acceptable. Each person will bring to him the level of communication which is suitable for him. Each person will be aware of what he needs for his development. As the person communicates that awareness mentally, that experience will be given to him in the way that is appropriate for him.

Question: Is all the electronic equipment around, an impediment to our growth?

You will be aware that the electronic age, as you are experiencing it right now, is expanding to such a degree that your planet is being bombarded with vibrations of such a nature that will ultimately cause interference waves that will impact on every living thing on your planet. These impact upon you as the Soul Being you are. They impact upon your psyche. They impact upon your own energy field. They cause in many ways distortions in your own thinking and feeling.

Equally so, they will have an impact upon much electronic equipment on your planet. As the years go by, low frequency vibrations, microwaves and interference patterns generated as a result of the multitude of radiations impacting on each other, will cause disease in animal and human life. Guidelines need to be established to monitor and maintain a regulation that will allow these systems to function in ways that will be less detrimental to human life. These will be more evident after the year 2000. Accidental deaths will occur, for example, with your aircraft because there will be so much interference in the countries over which the planes fly that it will cause malfunctions in the aircraft's electronic equipment. There will be a realisation of the areas around the planet which are at the greatest risk. Then there will be new guidelines. All of this is preparation for the ultimate when these types of equipment will be discarded in the future.

Forty to fifty years into your future, *you* will be such powerful electromagnetic beings, you will bring light, heat and all you require from within your own inner self, your own souls.

I am able to feel waves coming off electronic equipment now and I am sometimes not very comfortable.

You have been aware, when you move from a place where there are no electrical impulses, microwaves or radiation, into a place where they are, you will immediately feel the 'busy-ness' in your auric field, the interference patterns within you that cause distortions in your own thinking and feeling. There is a transformational process that is taking place. In the establishing of a global network, computer age information technologies will accelerate and continue to expand in a phenomenal way. This will continue for some time.

Concurrently, there will also be expansion and development of a greater degree of telepathic communication in the minds of those people who are developing alongside and ultimately expanding at a greater rate than the computer technology.

No need for external technology

At a time quite some distance ahead, there will no longer be a need for computers or any external communication technology, but for the moment they provide the transition phase because they are the external image of what will eventually take place internally. For a period of time the technological instruments of communication will become more and more specialised, more and more differentiated, more and more compact. Eventually there will be mind communication with these instruments so that when you sit at the computer you will have direct mind communication with it. Then there will be no need for the computer as an intermediary. There will be a direct line of connection. Realise that via a computer, through a connection in a wall and through fibres that travel across the oceans, people sense a global brain that enables a global communication to take place.

The idea of a global brain sets in motion the idea of a global brain in other realms. It then allows the technique of how to connect into a particular number or vibration, to enable the individual to connect with a person who has the number to which you wish to link. As you see the way to do this, that idea will create the ultimate whereby you no longer need the instrument. The global brain is already in place and it is already possible to telepathically connect with it.

Communication - tools and the human factor

Question: Must we become computer literate? Or are we going beyond the need for computers?

Both of those are relevant. Both are important. It may be important for you to have your motor vehicle until you learn to consciously travel (levitate) with your body, without the need of a motor vehicle. Remember when it was necessary to adjust to the demands of an industrial age. Again it is necessary to adjust to an information age, the age of the higher mind in transition. Trust the process. Transitions can be uncomfortable for those who are caught in between. It is the message to change. Those who are in harmony with the new age will seek to learn more, to experience more in the way of knowledge.

In the future, approximately 50 to 100 years for those who decide to stay on, you will be able to prepare your bodies for levitation. The changes in your DNA are already being activated right down to the cellular level to facilitate that ability. In the meantime, until such time as you have learned the power of the mind, the computers will be of value to you. Computers at this stage are still highly complex and large, but there will be tiny little computers that will be the size of a fingernail that can be influenced by your mind, in the years to come.

Rather than having your laptop computer which you carry around like a briefcase, you will basically have something that will be attached to you, very much like a wristwatch, and your own mentality will be able to attune to it. The components in it, as indeed are the components now, will be crystalline in substance and as you have learned to develop your mind in harmony, there will be the ability to link up to massive data banks with your mind. There will be the data banks on the physical, tangible level and also data banks you can access in the Akhashic Records. They are coming closer and closer together until in the future they will be as one and you will not need the tangible vehicle. We are talking about fourth dimension and beyond.

It is the expression in the physical world which enables you to make real those other dimensions *in* the physical world. You will not one day wake up with a set of wings, leaving this world behind, finding yourself in another world altogether! You are to create the transformation on this planet, to create all you require *on this planet*. That is why it is important to practise using the imagination. In your imagination, practise being the magician to create miracles through the image, belief and desire, then what you wish to have, will occur.

Many of the ideas of the past belong to the past. New concepts have not yet fully formed, nor have they descended into consciousness in a way which would allow you to feel what you are moving toward, for you are only catching a glimpse of the new dawning of the future. The future is what you are creating now in the visions, and in the image facilitated by the newly-activated pineal gland. Synchronicities are occurring because Uranus has moved into Aquarius and those of you who are Aquarians or who have aspects to Aquarius will feel the impact of that. When Pluto moves into such a very powerful house as Sagittarius, breaking down old structures and encouraging activation and expansion of new ideas, you will find major reformation, restoration, regeneration, and rejuvenation will take place against the backdrop of the conflict and turmoil of the past.

Initiations of water and fire

You will outgrow so many things in your lives. The urge to step into the new vision will be felt so strongly, yet at the same time the quicksand of the past will tempt you to stay where it feels familiar, until the Earth rocks you out of your complacency and the Spirit of the fire reminds you that you are spiritual Beings and you are going home! The Holy Spirit is the fire that, like the elixir, will open the way for you to be a miracle of creation, for the gifts of Spirit will be felt again, and those who have waited so longingly: "When will I be able to be a healer? When will I be able to create a miracle?" You will *do it* and do it again!

Next year (1997) will be a year of miracles. Next year will be a year in which as you decide, so it will be. And you will rediscover your spiritual families, and you will work with your spiritual families as a unit, to create even more miracles. For it is here that you will find the way to accelerate. You can no longer sit back and go for the ride. *You are the ride itself!* It is time to take up your power and to take the responsibilities of your purpose for being here. There will be for many of you the urge to realise your spiritual Self, to connect again with you, the Spiritual Being. This *is* your way home. It is the only way home.

Those who resist will delay their journey. Be willing to set aside the time to be with your spiritual family, those in the physical world, and those in the other dimensions. Spend time with each of them. Enter into the silence and listen, for you will hear them as you have never done before. The activation of the inner organs will facilitate, for all of you, the ability to hear, the ability to know, the ability to remember, to recall. You will amaze yourselves!

Emotions

In moving through these transitional changes, you will experience a multitude of emotions, a vastly different type of conscious state. With an expanded awareness you will perceive more life forms and see and experience what is beyond the third dimension. Consciously you will be able to hold the energies in a very different way. You will move through a transition which will take, perhaps, a period of twelve years. We speak here of the broader transition. The limited transition will take perhaps only three days.

During the twelve years transitional period, you will experience every emotion of which you can ever conceive, from fear right through to a feeling of absolute bliss. These you will experience in varying ways. We invite each of you to release and let go of fear. Fear will hold you back and will draw you away from full consciousness of yourself, back into your third-dimensional world. By relinquishing fear, you will embrace more of the higher levels of awareness. Your awareness will begin to shift consciously more into intuitive and inspirational levels. You will feel as if your left brain, the conscious, cognitive, rational way of working out problems, will fall by the wayside. You will feel less inclined to attempt to understand things in a rational and linear way. You will feel as if your memory is disappearing and you will only access that which is direct knowledge.

When you seek to go back in time, your memory will fail you and you will find yourself living a more present time existence with an expanded access to more resources beyond the conscious. Ultimately, all that you will have available to you is the concept of present time and the idea of thought, choice, and the image and the principles that will govern your immediate needs.

In the intuitive levels of awareness there will be conscious access to your higher Self. We encourage all of you to establish a conscious relationship and association with your higher Self. Your higher Self is a real Being, a Being more real than you are in the world in which you exist at present.

Marriage breakdowns

Question: There seem to be so many marriage breakups these days. Is this all part of it?

It is not a direct cause, but it is certainly part of the process. There are two principles at work here. One is what we will call equalising the energies of male and female, and the second is the change in value systems being strongly felt throughout your society, creating conflict within the family. This has also to do with the sense in which both men and women are becoming aware of their different focuses, different purposes and different needs in a relationship. Therefore they are determining what was acceptable to them in the past is not acceptable to them in the future. They are recognising that because life is of value, why stay in a situation that does not provide them with satisfaction on a soul level?

Some of you have been married twice, others even three times, or if you have never married, then similarly in the relationships to which you have committed yourselves. You will find that as you remember the person you were in the first relationship or marriage, you are not the same person. You are different, even if you look back over the last ten years of your life - quite dramatic for some of you. Others, who sat in front of the television, perhaps did not notice the changes going on around them: "What is it that I see? Is that a new human being?"

Longevity

You have not changed completely yet, however, in ten years of your life you are creating a body that will begin to glow from within. You are initiating an activation of the principle of Light so that the cells in your body that veil the light will change and your bodies will become more of the light bodies that they are. Then when you look in the mirror, you will see more of the beautiful colours, more of the light being that you are. You will realise that the light that comes externally to you, that flows into your brain, is releasing chemicals that will enable the changes to take place.

You are evolving a whole new species of human being. As you are moving forward there will be some who seem to be going faster than you. You will look to them and say: "My, you look *wonderful*. What have you been doing? Having a facelift? What has happened to your skin? It looks so good! What did you do?" They will reply: "It is the light." It is the beginning process which will accelerate in the next ten years in preparation for what will be a very obvious change in human shape and form in 100 years hence. Some of you may choose to stay and have a look. You do not have to depart when you turn ninety-five or even one hundred and ten!

You have read about those in your Bible who lived over 1000 years. Those who have studied the Bible say they must have had a different way of measuring time. Perhaps they measured by the number of times the moon went around. *That* (the light) is the reason. They really were that old, because they understood the secret of maintaining youthfulness and that is what you will discover in the years that await you.

Question: Is unemployment connected to the transitional period?

Yes it is. But do understand unemployment has always been a problem in some form. There have always been beggars in a society that does not honour the feminine energy. Your whole world as you know it is going through change. What has sustained employment in the past will no longer do so. What has been providing work for people in the past will no longer do so. The phenomena of change quickens and those involved in the decision-making are not yet in harmony with the change. They have not had the foresight, nor have they taken the decisions needed to provide the opportunities for learning, in harmony with the new focus and direction of a changing world. Those willing to acknowledge a new energy will redirect their attention and be willing to change.

It is most important that those with young children be prepared to point them in the direction of the energies. Be aware that there will not be the manual labours as there have been in the past. There will not be the incorporation of work on the farms as there has been in the past. There will be new skills for developing food and greater productivity in less space. Change is going to happen in every facet of life.

The Aquarian Age will set in motion a revolution within the work environment. New types of work will be created, such that all will be seen as valuable contributors and will be given the opportunity to express themselves according to their natural preference.

Personal initiation

We have come from afar to be with you. The great Spirit has called us forth to initiate within each of you the ideas that will prepare you more fully for what can be anticipated in your changing lives. As we speak with you, we would like to say that initiation is a process that each and every one of you has experienced in many lifetimes. Initiation is an acknowledgment of achievement. It is the final ceremony to honour that achievement. In by-gone periods, in different tribal situations, it was deemed that initiation would take place as the child became the adolescent and again as the adolescent became the adult. Initiation was a very strong and important component of what took place in the temples of old.

You are now moving toward an initiation of a different kind. All of you have been in the temples of old - the Grecian, the Mayan, Atlantean, Tibetan or Egyptian. Each of these required the honouring of the initiate, the honouring of the priestess or the priest. Each person in the testing needed to be challenged on very, very deep levels. One of the initiations required the neophyte to be placed in the sarcophagus in the Great Pyramid and remain there for a period of either three days or a half cycle of the moon, depending on the degree of initiation. The neophyte would leave his body and travel to a specific place to meet the Elder teachers. On his return he would be tested by the priests or priestesses to determine what he had learned. The initiations you will be going through will have a similar impact as that on the neophytes of old. Those particular practices were a little on the barbaric side, though not quite as bad as many others that preceded them! There were activities that were quite horrendous, and each had the purpose of creating the idea of pain and activation of enlightenment, all at the same time. We mention this for specific reasons. Each of you will find the idea of pain and suffering will no longer be a part of your particular reality in the transitional period ahead. Pain will no longer be required in any way, shape or form.

So when we say you will be going through an initiation, it is the preparation for that transitional time, between moving from human to the spiritualised human. We would hesitate to say 'super human' because you might anticipate you will become like Superman. That is not what we are intending. You are moving from your human expression, which has been your image for so long, into a total change of identity. You will no longer identify yourself through the human body. *Really allow* yourself to take that in fully. We have talked to you before about developing and awakening your spiritual Self.

Neurotransmitters

We have said your initiations in the past included activating the endocrine glands in your brain, to develop specific abilities that were then required for the initiate. You are now living in a different time/space dimension and preparing to move into a higher dimension which will require different organs to perceive the change of time/space dimension. The pituitary and pineal glands, activated during this initiation, will release certain neurotransmitters. They will then create a transformation in your body, sufficient for it to quicken, sufficient for it to become lighter, more *enlightened*.

This initiation process began in 1995 and will continue in 1996 and 1997. As you move forward through those periods of time, you will realise that the year 1998 will be quite a phenomenal year in every way you can imagine.

Watch what is taking place in the Middle Eastern countries, for they have become the barometer of your planet, and therefore the barometer of you. As above, so below. As you see external, so you see internal. As there is conflict in the external world, so there is conflict within the individual. The Middle Eastern countries will experience a major change in 1998. The way is being prepared. It is moving like a pendulum - back, forth; back, forth; conflict, peace; conflict, peace. It is a bit like the left brain and the right brain. A little bit like not knowing whether to take action or to be peaceful and harmonious.

The Middle East will become very much of a barometer that will equate with what is taking place, not only for you the individual, but with the global situation, for it holds the key. We are saying this because the initiation you will go through will be catalysed, if there is such a word, by those countries in that region. It is there, holding the energy, holding the resonance of that ascension process, that transformation process. See it as if it were a mirror, a reflector, so it may be fed back to you: "In what way may I bring about changes within me? In what way may I bring more light into my system? In what way may I bring more peace into my life?"

As you do this you create the greater love, the greater peace that will go through to those areas. You cannot hasten this process that needs to have time, for you are still constrained by time and this third-dimensional world, but you can allow it to happen with greater ease for all concerned.

You are in the middle of a transition as you move from one dimension to another, from the death of the old, into the resurrection and ascension of the new. Jesus demonstrated an initiation process with his resurrection and ascension. His way was the transition from Aries into Pisces, the way of the martyr. Jesus carried his cross, was whipped, wore the crown of thorns, was ridiculed and tortured. It was not an easy transition. You will not be doing that. You will not need to go through what you would call bleeding knees, crawling as it were, "Save me from my sin!" You are to be initiated into the Aquarian Age!

You will move easily from where you are now, dependent on your desire to bring the greater peace, the greater light, the greater love into the cells of your body. Focus on the spiritual. Focus on being the greater expression of the spiritual Self and, as you do, you will facilitate an easy transition so that your initiation will be one of blessed ease. See the peace flowing out to the many places in your world that are endeavouring to bring about peace in their own way. It will spread more and more.

You will need to adjust. Your lives will be changing quite rapidly. You think you have everything stabilised. You thought you were to sit and be quite comfortable for a period of time, then all of a sudden, something else comes in and pulls the rug from under your feet again!

116

Then your life will go through another series of changes. Then you think: "This is it. This will be the change and I will just sit here quietly minding my own business." And the gods say: "Not quite ready" and pull the rug from under you again! You will cry: "My goodness, what is this all about?" We say to you that you will go through change after change after change. You will live five lifetimes in as many years. You will be growing so very fast, like a child turning into an adult in a very short period of time. You are becoming spiritual human beings in ways you have not considered before. Your world will rock, it will shake, rumble and roll, like any good dancer! It is the dance of life! Your planet will be moving through its own change, for it too is moving through this initiation into a new expression of itself. This spaceship, your planet Earth, is indeed going through the most amazing journey.

We will give you an analogy. You *have one sun in your sky. When the process is finished, do not be surprised if you find two suns in your sky! Do not be surprised if you find yourself journeying right through your present sun to find yourself in a totally different place in the universe. Do not be surprised if, when you look up to the night sky, the stars you see will be nothing like the stars you see now.*

Those of you who have read your ancient books of Egypt will be aware there was a time when the sun rose in a totally different direction. You will find an even greater change and it is to that end we wish to prepare you. You may say: "No, this is not going to happen. My life will continue." We invite you to believe that and hold on to that, and then we invite you to open your eyes a little more and just see how much your life is changing. Almost in spite of you, it is changing. You still have a few years yet before you complete the final decade of this millennium. You have risen to this great height. What happens when you reach the end? You will continue to expand and grow. Prepare yourself for the changes.

The oceans will be turbulent in your lives, aggressive and angry because of the changes and the adjustments. Do not be surprised if your emotions also become shaky, if you feel perhaps at times tears that you cannot understand. You will feel at times: "Why am I crying? I do not understand this. Why am I feeling so angry? Why am I feeling so on edge? Why am I feeling this unusual emotion?" These are all symptoms of the changing times. You will need to honour the depth of your emotions and their necessity in your movement forward into your spiritual awakening. The Aquarian Age is the age of the mind and it is also the age of the Soul.

Chapter VI
Extraterrestrials

Observers From Beyond

The Zetas

Humanoid Extraterrestrials

Abductions

Polentet, The Pleiadian, Speaks

CHAPTER SIX

Extraterrestrials

Extraterrestrials exist in many forms and in many dimensions. As many dimensions as there are, there are beings who live and dwell therein. Even in this third-dimensional world of yours, you look around you and see multiple forms of life that exist on *your* planet, from caterpillars and butterflies right through to various animals and fish in your oceans. There are many unusual forms. If you were to go into the oceans and forests you would see things that would scare you if you met them in your bedroom at night.

Equally so there are multiple dimensions and existing in each one there is a multiplicity of forms. Since they do not live on your Earth, you can refer to them as extraterrestrials. Even as you believe in microscopic forms, there are others so large and so vast that even your Concorde aeroplane will be seen as miniature in comparison to some of the beings that live external to your world.

The purposes for which the extraterrestrials come to your planet are many and varied. Many more have come than those with which you are familiar, whether you call them Pleiadian, Orion, Arcturian or Sirian. It matters not what you call them. There are multiple forms in which these beings exist and they have all influenced your planet in different ways. In the far distant past, many millions of years ago, your planet went through a major crisis. This was a time of galactic battles that created such havoc in the universe that this solar system, being a focal point, drew to itself a comet which displaced Earth from its position.

Influences from the Pleiades and several other extraterrestrial races created a change in the solar system that was so vast, its culmination required major corrections for the many races of beings who were living on Mars, Venus and the various moons around the outer planets. For evolution to continue, it was necessary for beings of a higher order to step in and make adjustments to planetary positions.

The moon was moved to its position around planet Earth to provide a balance between the force of the Sun and the other planetary influences. If this had not happened, life on Earth would have perished and all who were dependent on the planet to fulfil their ultimate purpose would have been denied the opportunity.

After Earth was moved into the position it now occupies, it became an ideal place for many visitors. It also became a very complex planet with very high level beings from other systems entering into primitive human forms.

At present, your planet is the dwelling place of many hybrid races who have come together to resolve their differences and align themselves with God/Goddess/All-That-Is.

You as individuals are beginning to wake up to your extraterrestrial ancestral origins. You are also waking up to the karma of those beings who now have the task of healing the wounds of past intergalactic battles now played out in miniature between the various races on your planet. Your planet is a major focus in both time and space. You as a humanity are phenomenal in your ability to resolve these differences in such a way as to create an explosive impact that will resonate throughout the universe. While you continue to experience the friction of those who attempt to sabotage, it is helpful to realise the powerful forces at work with the gift that was given you by the Luciferians, those light beings who were the fallen angels. With the gift of choice and decision you have the ability to create through belief and imagination.

Those beings from Orion, Alpha Draconis, Niburu and some from other planets who provide the regressive influence, are not able to understand the gift of conscious creation. Their technology requires machines and a superstructure that infiltrates your governments, monetary systems and, indeed, every facet of society. They use control and domination throughout humanity and create discord and disharmony to deliberately destroy the very fabric of society. They will come unstuck when the power of mind over matter confounds them; when they realise that the individual is becoming self-empowered and is no longer willing to be subservient to the superstructures that these ancient controlling beings have put in place.

The lesson for each is that even though you have entered into the third dimension of light expression (the most constrained and limited in time and space) you are still able to influence it through your beliefs and images. You will not need a technology. Your actions will be fuelled by your emotions and inspired by your dreams. You will be bathed in the light and love of God/Goddess to provide you with all the resources required to heal a past that is played out in the present.

You are the extraterrestrials of old. The voices that speak to you are those of your ancestral families and friends who have taken a different route. Perhaps they are there to remind you of your relationship together; of a time in the distant past when you were perhaps a survivor of Maldek[1], or when you were involved in a war between worlds and were cast out to a far planet to learn a new way of expressing yourself. Now you are waking up and realising your destiny in the transformation of a humanity that is ready to come home.

Observers from beyond

It is impossible to generalise, but ultimately realise that you as a human consciousness at this time are so highly evolved in so many ways that you have made the decision to participate in a process that has not ever been achieved before. So, you are being observed to discover how you will do that. Some of the observers are a little envious of the choices you have made, of the opportunities you have given yourselves. So, they seek in their own way to share your journey with you.

The visits will continue and will become more evident in the next few years. Those who have read the documentation, know there is more than sufficient evidence to suggest that the presence of extraterrestrials is known by people in authority. It is known by the

---

1 Maldek, a former planet of this solar system, destroyed in an ancient past.

Australian Government, the American Government and is very much in evidence and acknowledged by those in authority in other countries too. That information will be revealed in greater measure. Not only will their presence be revealed, but also their identity and purpose.

The Zetas

The Zetas, sometimes known as the Greys, are a hybrid race who have changed from their original form over many thousands of years. They are the survivors of a planet that was destroyed after they were infiltrated by the Orions and suffered at the expense of Orion intervention. Due to the fact that their planet could no longer support them, they went underground where they deteriorated physically to the extent of being unable to reproduce, digest food or relate emotionally in the same way humanity does at this time.

While the human race has an extreme of emotional expression, the Zetas, who were more human-looking originally, have none. They share a group consciousness, unlike humanity which has become totally individuated. They developed in similar ways to your insect kingdom, similar to a beehive mentality, in that they are sharing an internal infrastructure of a mind-base that causes them to create 'hives' in the ways they mentally accommodate each other.

The Zetas, capable of time travel, recognised their deterioration and the conclusion of their species and journeyed throughout the galaxy looking for a suitable home. Through their interactions with your governments they were able to exchange information for accommodation in remote underground places throughout your world. There are three places in Australia, one of which is Pine Gap. You may wonder what occurred on their planet to cause them to go underground. There was a massive war amongst many extraterrestrial species and the Orions were the victims of that battle. Their wounds were deep and their aggression heightened. There is nothing to compare on your planet at this time for you to be able to understand the total devastation that occurred. All life forms went through massive genetic

124

transformation. Those that survived found the surface of the planet was contaminated beyond recovery and it became a dead planet over time. That is why it was essential for the survivors to leave. The survivors experienced a number of different genetic changes and as a result were forced to find new ways of survival. All that was previously available was a threat to their very existence. They only survived underground because of their superior mind development and the ability to use their mind to regenerate their bodies.

The Zetas have discovered that their only way of evolving is to again unite and blend emotional expression into their genetic coding. So they have entered into your planet for that explicit purpose, to again bring into their genetic pattern the opportunity to love. During various periods of time they have come as observers of emotional expression in humans.

Those of you who have in their ancestry genetic links to the Zetas through the Orion influence will have a greater affinity, so they may seek you out. They sense and recognise the resonance that is genetically coded. It is perhaps similar in that some people born in Australia have a European or English ancestry. You could trace it back several hundred years and you would be able to say you have linked within your blood line a particular quality that is recognised and remains therein for thousands of years.

Humanoid extraterrestrials

There are many who walk amongst you who have a form which is humanoid in every way. They come and go for various reasons, blending with you to experience life as you experience it and to influence where they deem it appropriate. They did not come through a mother the way you did. They participate in earthly life in similar ways to you. Some may even work amongst you. Those known as Pleiadians move freely amongst you and you would not necessarily suspect their origin. Only those who were familiar with their specific characteristics would recognise them.

There is another race, sometimes called 'The Men In Black', who enter in from time to time to influence the consciousness of people in positions of authority. They have concern for the future direction of your planet and your people, yet, they can sometimes appear threatening when there is resistance on the part of certain individuals. Realise there are many dynamics which appear at cross-purposes. Do trust that the higher Order will succeed, even though at times there is sabotage by some who have entered in through the net of higher frequency protection that has been cast around your planet.

Abductions

We wish to speak to those of you who may have experienced abductions, either physically or astrally. Prior to your coming into this life, there was a mutual agreement on the astral and higher levels, a co-operation, to support an awakening humanity. It is only the interpretation of the experience on a conscious level that allows fear to be generated. Fear is one of the final frontiers to be crossed, resolved and healed before you may make the transition into the greater unification. Fears that many of you experience, from the small fears all the way through to the greater dread, are very much connected to genetic coding placed within you several hundred thousand years ago. The beings which entered into your planet at that time and genetically interfered by encoding fear into your chromosomal pattern, did so with the desire to control. They wished the growing, evolving human form at that time to be so afraid of them that they literally went too far. Those who had been mutated were so fearful that their only way of coping with life was to go underground. They went into caves and built internal cities for themselves.

Such genetic coding, when it is introduced into the human form, the human psyche, must ultimately be decoded. All of you will need to heal, decode, rescript and reprogram, so that fear is *no longer a part of your psyche.* We encourage you to face your fear, heal the cause of it, for it has its origin genetically when there was the first separation from your Source, from your spiritual union.

The initial reason for the interaction between your governments and the Greys was to enable an exchange of technology. It needs to be appreciated there are multiple dimensions of activity overlaid one on top of the other. You, who are involved in time, are not necessarily able to perceive the larger picture.

After such a global tragedy as World War II, it was necessary to accelerate the human consciousness to a very high degree as quickly as possible. Much of a destructive nature which was designed to lead to the physical destruction of your planet in a very short period of time had been set in motion. It would ultimately lead to the destruction of your human race. It was deemed necessary to have two streams of acceleration put in place. One was the acceleration of the spiritual and the activation towards Christ Consciousness. The other was the acceleration in your technologies in the areas which would awaken you to the greater beyond so you would transcend the idea of being the only ones in the universe. The major focus of all the technologies was towards that end.

Those who were the instigators and the preparers of the plan set in motion all that was required to enable the expansion of life, the establishment of programs to awaken consciousness and lift you out of your complacency. There is much to describe in this area, however, suffice to say in all situations there are those who enter the scene attempting to prevent the evolutionary cycle for their own benefit. The interactions will also benefit the Zetas, who are a very significant group of beings. Karmically (and we use that word only because you will grasp the concept of what we are saying), the greater negative impulses that were initially set in motion need to be healed now. The soul beings of the Zeta have been displaced for many hundreds of thousands of years and it is imperative those beings are given the opportunity to complete their relationship with themselves so that they may evolve their species back to its Source.

Those who had suffered during the genetic manipulations and continuous battles, will ultimately be given the opportunity to find their way home through the creation of a form that will be more conducive to providing the way home. There are several hybrid expressions on Earth in other dimensions. They are not quite ideal in their presentation and are still in transition. There will be sufficient influence from those who seek to assist them so that there can be a healing of all who have been traumatised. There are many who have been called into the playing field of the Zeta transformation, some seemingly against their will, yet, in the higher order this will ultimately be understood.

No human soul will be lost to the purpose of its own spiritual journey. Each has experienced sacrifice, or perhaps you would prefer another word. Do see the greater picture so you may value what is experienced for a higher purpose. From the human viewpoint you would perhaps see only the negative face, yet look at how your surgeons freely cut out portions of your body and discard them without consideration of the impact on the total body!

What has been done with those involved in abductions, whether physical or astral, serves many purposes. Those involved have gifted much and will ultimately gain much with the expansion of awareness and the development of compassion. We are not condoning invasion or abduction. We only invite each individual to see the message.

You may ask: "...and what of asking permission? We need to consciously give our permission!" We will reveal to each person in due course the reminder of his agreements. To reveal the agreements too soon before the individual has developed compassion would cause much trauma.

There are now sufficient numbers of Zetas who have been changed to enable the birthing of a new race of beings who will provide a rich soil in which to grow and develop their souls in ways which were not previously possible. There are only a very few of the original Zetas who have remained on your planet, sufficient to maintain the nurseries. But do understand this program has existed for 40 years and the early beings, of which there are only a few, have gone beyond the nursery stage. Those who have been successful in their adaptation are proving to have the necessary foundations for much emotional soul interaction and you may be assured that you, as a humanity, will meet those who you have so beautifully aided in their development. As they are an entirely different species, they will express in very different ways to you. They are already strongly telepathic. You have much to learn from them and in turn they will learn from you the strength of emotional love.

As human beings, to become One again with your spiritual heritage you must face and overcome fear. For most of you it will be one of the greatest challenges of your life. You will find in various ways you will be facing your specific fears over the next ten to eleven years. The greatest of all fears for humanity is the fear of love.

Question: What is the meaning of little triangular puncture marks I have found on my body? I only found them once on my husband in the space of 20 years, but have often found them on my children.

May we ask specifically where the puncture marks were located?

Sometimes around the heart area, the abdomen and sometimes on the shoulder. They are three red dots in a triangular formation.

We have spoken before of the tetrahedral shape. The puncture marks were placed on your body by beings who recognised your resonance, recognised you as a source of information and took samples of the bodily fluids, blood and lymph as well as etheric fluids, for they contain all of the elements which describe the totality of who you are. Taken and compared over periods of time, these were matched with each other and compared with your children. You and your children belong to the same ancestry and contain vital information necessary for them to be able to determine the ways in which you handled emotional situations in your lives. You were monitored according to the various experiences. If you were to go back, you would remember that these experiences often occurred at times during which there was a trauma that caused a change within you.

Yes, that is true.

This is part of the monitoring. Please realise that, rather than enter into a state of fear and helplessness, you can prefer to see you had agreed to be involved in an opportunity to supply information that would assist the evolving of a consciousness for the Zeta beings, of whom you are also an aspect.

Although you are at this point identifying yourself as only human, there will come a time when you will release the idea you are just a human. You will discover yourself as having existed and experienced in different forms, as varied as the fish in the ocean and the birds in the air. Thus are the variations of forms throughout your universe and you have experienced diversity in some of these forms.

Are there certain questions still unanswered for you?

I still feel invaded.

We recommend you assist yourself by taking a journey into the subconscious, the belief around invasion. If we may, we would go back to two separate periods of time when an experimental process was taking place. Both of these experiences were against your will.

In the first one you were taken captive. We do not wish to go into great detail, but you were very much aware and conscious during this process. There was a certain investigation done on your body and you were held, as it were, clasped in position, unable to escape. Your screams and cries for help were to no avail. There was a further experience that goes back again to a period when there was a desire to find the missing link. At that time much experimentation was done in taking the human form back to the animal to explore how the animal and human were linked together.

It was there in Atlantis that they did certain things to your body to cause it to go through change. You were taken captive and there were invasions of your body that were quite horrendous to you. They affected you as the woman you were then. So here you are now as a woman feeling as if you are losing your power and not being valued as the woman you are.

We invite you to find a suitable person to assist you to go back and claim back your power. Claim for yourself the right to say *no* and reclaim your body for yourself. In this way will you set yourself free and be able to see a greater sense of purpose and destiny. There are people in this room who will assist you.

How many are afraid of the night in case they see something? How many were afraid of ghosts as a child? If you were told they were in your room now, not only humanoids, but many vastly unfamiliar in form, and your eyes opened too quickly and you saw it *all*, it would be quite a shock to your understanding. Many of you have, for some unknown reason, become very egocentric in this, your Earth, assuming there is nothing else but that which represents the human form. Oh yes, you have entertained the possibility. You have the dolphins and the whales swimming in your ocean, and you know that they are not humanoid and you know that they have superior intelligence. They have the ability to access the full range of the spectrum.

You entertain the idea that possibly they are from extraterrestrial origins. Yet to conceive that there could be anything else that looks as different again as your dolphin does to the human..., we ask you to imagine for a moment, all the life forms on your planet. We ask you to imagine the reptilians, the birds that fly in your air and the various others of your animal kingdom and to realise that they are, in many ways, the remnants of those that have visited your planet in other times, in other places. They have created forms as replicas, certainly somewhat remote from their original expression, having that expression of themselves to give you the idea that there is a consciousness that is not human in the way you understand human to be.

Polentet, the Pleiadian, speaks

Who are the Pleiadians? Well now, where to begin? It is a long story and too complex to summarise in the way that would make ultimate sense. As you cast your gaze out to the heavens you will find us in the constellation of Taurus. That is why you hold the cow sacred.

The horns of the cow are similar to the crescent moon and represent the great feminine principle and the great Mother as the source of life-giving light and warmth. We came into our prominence during the Taurean Age of your most recent time, where our foundations were laid in many countries of your world. We have been interfacing with humanity and influencing your evolution for many hundreds of thousands of years.

We are one of the most important stellar groups, along with Sirius and the Great Bear, in the Solar Logoidal system. As the Great Triune group we are the source of power behind the twelve zodiacal constellations, who in turn influence the solar system through the mediation of the Solar Logos. We have often been called the sisters or wives of the Great Bear. Alcyone is our brightest star and the centre of the universe. We are also mythically connected to the dove which is the emblem of the Holy Spirit. The dove is sacred to Venus and Aphrodite and we value that symbol as the great messenger of wisdom and power of the great Goddess who seeks to take care of her young.

As you would be willing to understand on a deeper level, we have now come into your world as messengers who wish to speak to you in a very strong way. We carry ancient codes, which are also relevant for your present time. Our message for you now is to take care of your children and your Mother Earth. Only then will she sustain you in her embrace as you move forward into your multidimensional expansion.

Question: What has been your recent involvement in our world?

To see that our recent involvement in your *world* began with significant people. We use that term because we wish to describe some of those interactions so you will understand what we mean. We will only describe what is known at this time for we still have influence in the lives of prominent people who have specific roles to play.

Now we will expand on this rather obscure beginning.

You will recall that, prior to your last World War, your world was in many ways very retarded in development. Your technology was very primitive compared to the standards of the Pleiadians. It was seen as an essential part of humanity's development to create new opportunities for expansion in the technological area.

We were involved in making contact with such members as Nikola Tesla, Wilhelm Reich and Billy Meier. These you will certainly know about, yet there are also others in positions of prominence in your scientific, entertainment and political arenas.

We had deemed it important to influence in several ways. It was necessary to bring about a process of awakening humanity to the knowledge of our presence. We have chosen quite a number of contacts throughout your world since the 1940's. They have responded in different ways to our interactions with them. For those whose task was simply to inform others of our presence there was not a great deal required of them except for the necessary exposure that our presence in their lives created. It was our intention to prepare the consciousness of humanity so that you would be ready for the expansion of your world into its new expression.

We needed to begin in the 1940's to take advantage of the forty year cycle to which your world responds. You will recall the significance of the number forty in many of your biblical texts. Secondly, it was necessary to contact those who were of a scientific nature so they would hasten technological developments in your world. We entered into agreements with people in your governments from the early 1940's, even though we were very present even in the 1800's. It was done initially to be seen as beneficial to the governments' war efforts, but it was our intention to use that need for what was to be a greater purpose.

We have participated in your planet's history and your humanity for thousands of years. We have also been involved in laying certain foundations in place from the very beginning of your planet's history.

Our involvement has not always been for the good of Earth's people, for in times past we have had selfish motives and were warlike, without scruples. We have been involved in long past battles with the Sirians, the Orions, the Draconians, the Titans and many

133

others. We were not involved with mutations in the way others have been. Rather, have we looked further afield from our own origin to find a playground to explore for our own purposes. Our major mistake of recent times was meddling in the affairs of a humanity that had charted its own course. Our interference created deviations that ultimately contributed to a downfall of human consciousness. Your most recent of world wars was created for a specific purpose and was again at the instigation of the ancient participants of interstellar battles who still struggle for supremacy on all fronts. We feel great regret for what has occurred, perhaps more correctly *how* it occurred.

The Philadelphia Experiment and the Montauk Project were also influenced by Pleiadians. We began our involvement with Tesla, a decision which was taken with great deliberation and care. Yet, we did not consider the human factor of greed and the desire for supremacy. Tesla held true to our guidelines, but others attempted to influence him into participating before the appropriate corrections had been made. When Tesla refused, another was appointed to take his place. This person did not have the necessary skills nor the ability to attune to the higher vibrational frequencies to receive the necessary guidance. This experiment would have succeeded if there had been even a slight delay. It was necessary to align the human factor with zero point, yet, when this was not possible, we and the Sirians attempted to delay what was to take place. There was a ripping of the fabric, yet again, to open the way so that it was then possible for many thousands of other extraterrestrial influences to enter in through that tear. That is how the Zetas or Greys and their counterparts were able to enter in such large numbers from the period of 1945 onwards.

You will recall a previous time in Atlantis where the fabric was torn. Those beings from Mars, originally Orion/Zeta hybrids, were behind both of those events. We had not anticipated the shocking impact on your world, for we had not considered that humanity would follow and not heed all the warnings that were given in regard to the timing of such an event. The Montauk Project was created to correct the mistakes which occurred during the Philadelphia Experiment.

These corrections were absolutely essential. It is now our task to clear the effects of that traumatic event, which took over forty years to return to normal. Now all is in order to facilitate the greater purpose. We have recognised there is a price to pay when one goes against Divine purpose. We have agreed to participate with others who were involved in our ancient battles so that we can correct the wrongs.

We have been persuaded by the Galactic Command to allow our involvement to begin the process of regeneration. As with all created species, there are those who are renegades and those who seek the highest and we have chosen now to make available our vast resources so that you as a humanity can hasten your evolution. We are also aware we have not always seen the error of our ways. You will be able to look back over the past 4,500 years and see two major streams of our influence. One stream has provided an educational information foundation deemed necessary for those who turned their backs on technology and wished only for self-development and awakening to the great beyond. Here lies access to universal libraries with information that has only just begun to filter through into consciousness.

The second stream is that of the scientist who seeks to extend the boundary of matter and the physical realms. We have achieved much in the field of technology and our involvement with your world has been quite phenomenal in the past forty years. We will continue to influence, for you have not reached your full potential in many areas. We will support those endeavours and at the same time we will prepare you for the acceptance of our presence in your world.

Question: Would you please discuss the role of the Pleiadians in the coming changes?

The Pleiadians have now developed to such a degree that they are able to participate with the Sirians, the Andromedans, the Arcturans, the Master teachers and the Galactic Federation to assist in awakening consciousness and accelerating the progress toward ascension. They came to this planet many thousands of years ago. Originally, they were known as the Bird Tribes. They love to fly. They have their connection to many American Indian tribes, both North and South.

Pleiadians also bring forth the energy of the Greek influence, that of the Olympic Games, that of embracing the beauty of Life and the value of the human form and its development to its fullest potential in all areas. They show love and beauty can be demonstrated in art and music and in the healing forms, which they represent. They bring forth balance and harmony in ways in which they can touch people. Know too, that each of you in your own way, connects to the Pleiadian spirit, however, it is for you to determine the ways and the degree to which you do.

Those who carry the greatest degree of connection to their Pleiadian source will be those who are very happy to live their lives fully and totally, exposed so all can see who they truly are. Remember, they are here to assist in the transformation of a humanity as part of their karmic responsibility. They will provide information in a variety of different ways and through a number of different channels.

Question: How will they (Pleiadians) interact with us as humans? What role will they be playing? Will they be teachers?

They will interact with you more specifically than they have done up until now, giving guidelines, but, not taking over to the degree that some have thought. They will give will give an overview of potentials and information that will expand consciousness beyond its limited perspective. They will provide possible solutions and will not interfere in the way those solutions can be implemented. Their task is to reveal to humanity what lies beyond the third-dimensional world and to expand awareness in preparation for the time of transition. They encourage the living of life more fully and in total harmony with nature. As necessary, they provide warnings when you as a humanity have deviated from your path of destiny.

The information will be disseminated in many ways. There has already been literal physical interaction. Now there are aliens walking amongst you. They walk in your streets taking up positions in certain places in this country and others in your world. They are situated where they are for a purpose. They will also give guidance as to how the information of their presence is to be revealed. For example, it has been decided, in group meetings between the aliens and those of Earth, on the best ways in which information could be presented to prevent massive fear. It has been suggested that your entertainment arena would be the best medium to present their presence, initially as fiction, then with certain programs on a regular basis to introduce the idea of their presence. Then, it will be tested from time to time. They will appear more frequently, perhaps with one ship, perhaps with many ships, over a particular area to gauge the acceptability.

Extraterrestrials have been interacting on many levels and in many stratas of society since the late 1800's. They have had regular meetings with government officials, especially during times of war and have assisted in the resolution of many conflicts. They have certainly prevented the outbreak of what could have resulted in the total destruction of your planet.

There is a destiny put in place by human consciousness and at the same time there are those who would sabotage that destiny. Some extraterrestrial beings have the task of monitoring, to ensure that destiny is fulfilled. At times when the missiles have been fired accidentally in such a way that would have destroyed the planet Earth, or a whole grouping of people in a major city on your planet, they have stepped in. On many occasions, too many, they stepped in to prevent disaster. At the same time be aware there are still a very few on your planet who represent something like your own negative egos, who are attempting to sabotage, to create traumas and tragedies. They will not succeed, but they do behave something like a rash on the skin, causing you to itch from time to time.

Beyond the year 2000, it will become more acceptable to allow the idea of a humanoid alien on your planet. The next step will be to accept those who do not appear in the same manner and guise as you do. It will take a little bit longer. What is required is a consciousness that comes from the heart. The greater consciousness of humanity still has a closed heart and that is affecting the total acceptance of those who would come to assist.

Chapter VII
Your Spiritual Family

Guides

Interdimensional Beings

Angels

CHAPTER SEVEN

Your Spiritual Family

You are assisted at every stage of your journey by a very large and all-encompassing spiritual family. You have travelled throughout all of your many lives together, both within your present spheres of comprehension and beyond into other galaxies in your universe.

Your spiritual family, for the most part, has its expression in the realms beyond the third dimension, yet, at the same time you will also have a very physical and very present group of friends around you who also comprise your spiritual family. These may not necessarily belong to your birth family, though it is possible some members of your immediate family will also comprise your spiritual family. You will always recognise them by the strong heart connection you feel toward each other.

Your other-dimensional spiritual family has elected to travel with you as you move forward into the fourth dimension and beyond. Even before you were born in this life-time, and as far back as your decision to enter into an exploration of the physical worlds, your spiritual support team made the decision to participate with you in a way which would be mutually beneficial to all concerned.

You will gradually draw to you, with increasing conscious aware-ness, those who you know to be of your spiritual family. We wish you to be clear about the concept of spiritual families.

Your spiritual family may be those who live and dwell with you on the third dimension, those you know to be your support team. Those are the ones you feel you may telephone, to talk about the changes taking place in your life, to share and commiserate with, to have the feedback and understanding and reflection, and who give the support that a spiritual family will enable you to have. Your spiritual family does not necessarily include your blood line family. It can include mother, father, brother, sister, but more frequently it does not. Your spiritual family comprises the ones with whom you resonate, blend and harmonise most. You do not have to join a club or organisation. You do not need to participate in a commune, sharing bathrooms together. You do not need to build a fence around your particular group of spiritual family.

That spiritual family can also include those who live in another country, who are supporting and encouraging you. They align with your personal dreams and visions for your future, and you in turn are there to assist in the creation of their future. Your spiritual family is not to be a family you can project onto, in the desire to have a mother or a father, or someone to solve your problems for you. This spiritual family is not to be seen as those who would maintain the idea of 'I have to be in charge. I have to be in control. I have to do it *my way*. I just want to tell you what has to be done.'

This family treats everyone equally and recognises the creative process. You, as individuals, will reach out with your minds to find the ways that you can more fully nurture and nourish those who are your spiritual family. You will possibly have friends to whom you feel close who are not necessarily spiritual family. There will be others you might ring on occasions and arrange to meet for that special intimate talk, for you know you have a way of communicating together which nourishes the soul and provides intimacy and support. In that manner, you will be able to discern the difference between a friend who is not of your spiritual family, and one who is, but not necessarily classified as someone with whom you would go out to see a movie.

In a similar way, as you have the horizontal line of family, you also have the vertical line. The vertical line of your spiritual family includes certainly your soul and your spirit. They are certainly your spiritual family. You cannot go anywhere without them! They may tag along because you have not yet owned them completely. They may be tucked somewhere in the crevices of your own unconscious because you have not yet released them. They are *you* and they are part of your spiritual family.

Be aware that those who are more directly in communication with you are your personal guides, who have a life of their own, independent and separate from you, and are unique and beautiful beings. You may communicate with them in the depths of your meditations until such time as you form that interaction and know they are there for you. You can drive your motor vehicle along the highway and know they are with you in the car. You can have a heart to heart conversation with them, knowing they are of your spiritual family and you can confer together. You will hear them communicate with you. You may share your dreams and ideals and they will share theirs. It may be, they can shed more light on your dreams and in that way, as the resonance comes together, you will create your future in the ways in which you hold the equal image and move forward.

As part of your spiritual family, you will have heard of the idea of soulmate: "Oh, my soulmate, that other half of me which I have lost throughout the ages."

There is that combination of a grouping of beings who have through lifetime after lifetime travelled together. You belong to that minority who represent the leading edge, always getting yourselves into trouble because you stretched beyond those who were behind. You were always the ones to be burned at the stake, thrown into the dungeons and tortured because you were showing the Light, speaking the Truth, belonging to spiritual communities or studying under the auspices of the greater teachers. Within that spiritual wave of which you are a part, there are some who belong to the same Oversoul, who share under the same umbrella of the Teacher. Perhaps the teacher is Zarathustra, Buddha, Krishna, Melchizedek or Pythagoras. Perhaps they are of the Tribes of Israel. Within those you will find that group which resonates with you, the family with which you have travelled along the highways and by-ways of lives.

Some of those are not in a body at this time, though they support you and are part of your Inner Plane spiritual family. As you go into meditation, invite them to come and be with you in that sacred place you create. Surely they will then come and join with you and you will have a round table conference! You will honour each other as to the gifts you have, and the creative ideas, and you will share the vision of a future that is to be, a world which is yet in the making.

Above and beyond those who are a part of your Earth plane there are those you call extraterrestrial. Extraterrestrials! We like saying that word! In a sense you are all extraterrestrial. In varying degrees you have all come from beyond this planet Earth, and you have created for yourselves a spiritual family which includes those who have their expression beyond your planet and share with you on other realms in the multiplicity of dimensions that are available.

You may include within your spiritual family those who resonate with you and with whom you share a common heritage. You perhaps sense there is a star up there, or even two or three, which seems to call you. When you look to the heavens you will say to yourselves: "That is my home" and we will say: "*It was.*" Your home now is where you are coming to. We emphasise, it is the removal of the veils between the dimensions which will create the idea that you are more than you consider yourselves to be at this time.

You as a humanity are evolving a whole new species. You as a humanity are evolving a species which has never been before; throughout all the galaxies of your universe there has never been a species like unto that into which you are evolving. You have come of age. You are now preparing for the greatest transformation of all times. Connect with those people with whom you feel most in harmony, for example, you may meet on a regular basis once per week or once every two weeks, once every month, in order to share visions, dreams and ideas together, to focus on areas which seem to need attention in your world and to create new concepts to resolve your traumas.

Your spiritual family may extend even further in that you may decide to take up residence together and work together. This family may create a teaching temple of light, of love, of wisdom, or focus on the environment. There will be any number of factors you may care to consider. There are no limits, only that each of you in your own way comes to an agreement of what is important to the group.

You may wish to consider how to increase the number of trees on the planet. The beginning phases are simply communication, finding those people with whom you personally feel compatible and offering an invitation. Those who feel comfortable will join you. It may change over time.

Guides

Every one of you, without exception, has two personal guides, a male and a female. It is necessary to have one of each to enable you to experience the qualities of each gender. There may be some amongst you who would prefer to deny you have two, or would rather say you only have a male or a female guide. If so, then it may be necessary to look at your own issues with regard to your parents and ask to what degree you are not able to embrace your mother or your father. Perhaps you have negated women or perhaps you see men as being too threatening and so will not allow one or the other of your guides to be available to you because you have not yet resolved your issues.

As well as your personal guides, you also have other guiding influences or angelic beings who come to share in your growth. These often have specific roles to play and you may ask them when you make your connections with them. It is possible for your personal guides to appear as light in your room. By your very sense, you will be able to discern the difference between your guides, an angelic presence or an extraterrestrial who has come to attend to you.

Inter-dimensional beings

Inter-dimensional beings are those who exist beyond form. They do not have a body in the way you understand bodies. Whether you exist in your third-dimensional world with a dense physical body, or on the fourth or fifth dimension, your body will still have a form, albeit vastly different in expression.

Those who have released the need to have a body form express through the essence of light only. They simply express through the ability to change the light body according to their specific needs and circumstances.

There are many billions throughout the myriad of galaxies in your universe who chose not to become directly involved in planetary existence. Rather, they have the task of overseeing the interactions between the various star systems and their inhabitants.

Now, there are extraterrestrial beings who have learned to project consciousness into this space where you presently have your expression. You would see them as a manifestation of light. Should they choose, they can also create a form to enable you to see them. Unless you have the ability to lift your frequency to that higher level, you will not see them with your physical eyes. Only those who are capable of seeing with their other eyes would see these beings.

Angels

Question: Can you please explain angels to us?

Angelic beings have been involved with Earth since before you existed as a human form. We of the angelic realms participated in this planet before it became physical. The densest of our realms was the etherium of which our body and that of the Earth was created at the time of our cycle. We have now evolved beyond the need for any form, as you understand form to be, but we remain within the resonant vibration of Earth for we have always been part of her journey and so also a part of yours. We have always been with you to shine the light and to give the radiance of our love, so each in your way may be encouraged to go forward into the greater light. We are Light beings and you may see us as brilliant light. We have often been called 'man made perfect' as we belong to that wave of evolution which went before you. When we went through an ascension, it was with an ease, very different from yours. We did not have to contend with the third-dimensional constraint with which you are working at this time.

When we went through the lowest expression of our form, an astral form, we did not create for ourselves a third-dimensional body. Some of us, as angelic beings, made the decision to be mediators and messengers. We have learnt to carry the messages from you to the higher realms and from the higher realms to you. Our light and love shine upon you so that you might be encouraged always to walk within the light and to feel you are surrounded by the light.

That we went before you does not mean that we are better. It means that we are different from you. You will move through the cycle as we have done and that cycle will also be followed equally by the other kingdoms of nature, the animal, plant and mineral kingdoms. Each in its own life cycle of expression enables the consciousness to expand and grow. So we are here to talk to you, to share with you the visions we see. We see your world very differently from the way you perceive it and we see you very differently also.

We wish to tell you about the light in the transformations that are taking place. Your planet is beginning to radiate. It is beginning to become radiant from its soul!

Your planet is moving toward becoming its own star. The outer planets in your solar system are not physical in the ways your Earth is physical. Neptune and Pluto are radiant in that they give forth a light and a heat from within the very essence of their beingness. Those planets are conscious as your Earth is conscious. The consciousness of those planets has developed to such a degree they radiate from the very being that they are. Your planet Earth has a consciousness that is beginning to radiate from within itself.

We watch with wonder and awe for we know also when that occurs. You will also bring forth a light from within your souls, from within your hearts. There are many of you who are concerned there will be a darkness that will come upon your planet, a void of blackness. The idea of the void and blackness creates fear within the souls of many. When your Earth expands in her consciousness she will shine forth her own light. She will have no need of the light of the Sun or of the day and the night for she will be her own light.

There have been periods of time in our past when we have watched and seen the nature of certain human beings who have become Masters of their time. A Master is one who is able to create his own light from the very essence of his being. They become radiant in their light expression. You will see them for they will glow in a particular way.

"There, surely, walks a Master" you will say. It seems almost as if their feet do not touch the ground, for they seem to walk in a different vibration. The true Master is one who has also mastered gravity, who has also mastered the elements of physical existence.

Each of you will eventually become a Master, some even in this very lifetime in which you live. You are finding the ways, albeit somewhat like an infant attempting to walk. You are attempting to learn to master this element of matter. It is a process that for some of you seems so very difficult. We smile as we watch, and we say: "Come now, here is a message for you to assist you to become a master." You are beings of Light, but your light is clouded by the very thing you are learning to encompass and embrace. You deem matter to be not of light. You deem matter to be negative and somewhat non-existent. Matter is made of light. All things are made of light. When you understand you are here to master this physical world, then, and only then, will you too shine your light from the very essence of your being. The light that shines forth from you will be seen by many. Then you too will know how to walk on water, to still the wind, to calm the fire and to change water into wine. Then as the spiritual being you are, you will shine forth and there will be no darkness, for you will have the light within you.

To give you an example: were you to step into a darkened room with your light, the room would not be dark. That inner light is so very powerful. You will have that potential given unto you very soon. We say a potential. It is for you, in the years you are moving toward, to live the principles of life and to understand the relationship that you have with the elements of your planet.

You have four elements - earth, air, water and fire. That is all. That is all there is on your planet. It is the combination of those four which together creates your body. Your physical body is of the mineral kingdom, the blood and lymph the fluidic, the air you breathe is of the element of air and the fire is the spirit that animates the body to give conscious awareness and choice.

To return to your question about angels: Yes, you have a story, a fairytale story of Hansel and Gretel, where they did leave the crumbs to find the way home. You too, are reading the signposts and you are finding your way home, however, you will not be following the crumbs that you left behind from a by-gone era, oh certainly not, for the way home is not the way you have been. The way home is a different way. We watch with such delight because you are moving ahead of yourself, across a terrain that has not been traversed before. You are creating your own signposts and we watch you! We give you the messages and you interpret them according to the directions in which you wish to go.

We are often called 'the wayshowers', and 'man made perfect'. We have been called by many names, but we will always be known as the Holy Host of Beings.

As we do not have a voice as you do, our means of communication would be felt in your soul, like a dancing light which sings a tune, and it is the tune that is experienced within your heart that carries the message. And so, we sing a tune to you and let the message be felt in your soul. We have prepared the way even though we travelled a different pathway and the light we have gained in our journey we now offer unto you.

We were in attendance when the ancient and Christed Ones made their transition. Always we have been there, for we stand at the Gates to usher in those who are about to make the transitions. Even when the Master Jesus was born we were in attendance and welcomed his presence and even when Mohammed and Buddha made their entrances, our light shone upon them and ushered their souls into expression. As they emerged in their own transition from that expression into the great Beyond, we were there again, shining our light that they might feel and know our welcome, that our presence was with them.

So we gather and we surround you, for you too are making your transitions. Many of you are aware of the great interest that has been developing around your world with angelic beings. You have talked of angels and your personal guardian angels. We would hasten to say to you that there is an angel for all occasions and there is an angel that looks after all situations. Even your United Nations has an angel that gives support and encouragement. Oh yes, we know to what degree we are permitted, or not permitted, to interfere in the unfolding and a breaking down of the old ways. It is our light and our love that encourages the breaking down of the old in order to bind together and link the fabric of what is new.

In our natural form we have no need of form or wings, for we are pure essence of light. You would perhaps see us as no larger than a small ball. You may see us as above your bed when half asleep in the middle of the night or in the corner of your room. You may think you see an illusion of light and we say to you we are not an illusion of light, we are the *real* light. Because we have often been misunderstood in our form of a sphere of light, multiple in its content and expression, we have chosen to manifest in the way that would give credence to how angelic beings have been described and so we do accommodate your desire to see the wings.

We offer ourselves to you in this form so you may know us in a way that will feel comfortable for you. We are a sphere of light as large or as small as we need to be. In all forms, small or large, we are never diminished in our capabilities; neither are you in the true essence of who you are. You too, are spheres of light, so very large, and yet so very compact. You are like the nucleus of a cell, the very core, for in that nucleus all is contained. We encourage you to be aware of your Allness and that the nucleus contains all of the information.

When we travelled with some of you across the desert sands in the exodus with Moses, we sometimes presented as a pillar of fire. At other times we chose to express differently, although we were always the one guiding principle that showed the way. And so we offer ourselves to you at this point of transition. As the newly born seeks to hold the hands for support, we too offer our hands to support you as you are being born into the new world.

When your eyes are opened at birth and you look around with awe, and see the giants of parent, of medical doctor or nurse, and see the grandness of size, you too, born into the new world, look around you also and will see with newly-opened eyes, the grandness of a being who stands tall before you, who seeks to support you until you become familiar with how to live in a world that is so very different.

It will take some time to adjust to what is to come. Fear not, Beloved Ones, for we are there to support you in your transition. In the time to come, you will understand the message of which we speak. Perhaps we speak prematurely, however we do speak to you in such manner as will enter into the core of your soul, stored away for future reference when the memory of what we have spoken of tonight will resurface, and you will find comfort in the words and will feel safety in the embrace of our love and our light.

Chapter VIII
The Sirians

The Sirian Vortex
God/Goddess
Cetaceans And Sirius

CHAPTER EIGHT

The Sirians

The Sirian vortex

We also take the liberty to speak with you about the Sirian constellation so you may appreciate the vastness of what that particular vortex means. We would like you to imagine Sirius as a vast portal or doorway. We wish to go beyond the concept of God as portrayed by your religious institutions and also remind you that the universe in which you live is only one of many millions of universes. The words "In the beginning God created" are particularly relevant when we speak of Sirius. Your own particular universe was created through the Sirius vortex. That particular portal is the doorway through which all of the cosmic energies from beyond this universe poured in.

You may compare your universe to a huge bubble or a womb into which the energy of God/Goddess flowed. Sirius holds the original archetypes that are expressed in the major arkana of the tarot cards. It also holds the energy of the sixty-four hexagrams of the I Ching. In truth the Sirian constellation holds the resonant vibration of the foundations of creation in your universe. It is here you will find the archetypal Mother, Goddess, Priestess and your soul. You will also find the archetypal Father, God, Priest and the foundations of mind or consciousness.

Sirius has a particularly significant relationship with Earth and this even more so at this period in your own personal transformation. While there are many who will tell you the changes you go through at this time are because of the precession of the equinoxes, or because the Mayan calendar is coming to an end, we would rather say to you that an event has taken place that is far greater than anything that has ever occurred in your universe before. We will explain the significance of this event by going back into the distant past.

Over 200,000 years ago the vortex of the Goddess into your Earth was invaded by those who were not in harmony with the greater purpose on planet Earth. Over time, the various beings who entered Earth created such terror and trauma that it was deemed necessary to make corrections to facilitate a gradual return to normal. Approximately 90,000 years ago, it was decided to close the Sirius portal except for a fifty-five day period from each 23rd of July when Sirius rose a minute in front of the Sun in the sign of Leo. The Sun is a vortex or portal into your solar system. When Sirius rises at such close proximity to Earth and the Sun, at a time when Sirius is at its closest to Earth, the energy released from the Goddess is so powerful that each year it causes the flooding of the Nile. This event was recognised by the Egyptians and was the reason why they have long since worshipped Sirius. It is also the reason why all of the temples along the Nile are built facing the light of Sirius. The yearly inflow of the energy of God/Goddess through the Sirius portal for only fifty- five days each year, has maintained the level of light and love of God/Goddess to assist humanity to awaken and transform itself in preparation for this specific period of time. Your whole universe, including the suns in each of the galaxies, is moving into an alignment like a formation dance. The correct configuration is needed to facilitate the changes within you, as individual beings of cosmic light. You are to awaken and become co-creators of a new spirituality.

We will use an analogy. A key that you put into a door has a particular shape or configuration. When it is turned in the lock, if it is the right key, it will release the lock and the door can be opened. Similarly, a combination code has been created, a galactic configuration incorporating planetary systems within your Zodiac. The activation of that process took place in the sector of Scorpio in April of 1994, to activate the feminine space and allow the feminine/Goddess energy to flow. The planet Jupiter moved into the correct configuration to activate the code. The comet Schumaker-Levy IX was also part of the dance, entering into Scorpio and impacting upon Jupiter to be the great messenger in the sky pointing the finger to where the action was taking place.

Beyond your perceptions, other alignments happened that included those vortices of the suns of Sirius, A and B. These entered into and became part of the code to align in such manner as when each was brought into the total and correct configuration, a signal pulsed through the universe, poured down through those channels and activated so that the door would be opened. With the activation and the opening, the beginning stages of what would lead to a total transformation of human consciousness began. That impact will enable the human being to be transformed into the spiritualised human being. Realise that Sirius is a direct doorway into this universe, as it is also a doorway out of the universe. There is a particular energetic spiral that is created and established by virtue of two different frequencies of energy spiralling between Sirius A and Sirius B, which sets up a third component similar to a tetrahedral shape. That is the inter-universal point which will allow those who seek to travel beyond this universe to find it as a doorway or access way. Some may perceive it as a Black Hole that would catapult them into dark space through to the other side and so to find their way home again. Now the way has been opened for the energy of God/Goddess to again pour down in a measure equal to what it was prior to its closure. The Goddess is being born again, yet your experience of Her will be uniquely yours.

God/Goddess, who is not a Being in the way you would ever understand a Being to be, is vast beyond measure and infinite in complexity. The component characteristics or qualities from God/Goddess flow through that vortex, stepping down into your own galaxy, then to your own solar system and to planet Earth, and then to each and every heart and mind throughout the world.

God/Goddess

You will experience God/Goddess as love and light. These are words that have become empty of meaning by the many who would seek to use them without the fullness of understanding of what they truly represent.

The light is a light like no ordinary light. Its frequency of vibration is higher than anything else in your universe. The Law of Resonance is at work and because this light is so high, it will draw everything else into harmony with it. The light of God/Goddess is also a light that holds within it the memory of everything that has ever occurred throughout the totality of your universe. It contains the light of all wisdom. It is a light that lightens. We use the word 'lightens' in its many diversities - to add light, to become enlightened, to add light to change the vibration so that the frequencies can be much finer.

The God/Goddess loves you and all of humanity. The God/Goddess pours her light upon you, yet surely She would not do so in a manner to cause you harm, or give you more than you can contain or process. So it is that she measures according to what you are capable of receiving. Her light touches your soul, touches your heart, your mind and every cell of your physical body. It has specific components, for it too is a coded vibration. Every aspect of that light has a quality that knows exactly its task. In each of you throughout your planet the light from God/Goddess will activate specific chemical releases in the brain to shift and change in such a manner as to create new pathways in the brain. This will enable a change in thinking to release what has been blocking the way. The light of Goddess is a consciousness that is wise beyond measure. Equally, as the light flows, so too does love. The love is like a great magnet that unifies and draws unto itself all who are loved, without exception. The great Goddess loves. Her love, blended with light, provides the opportunities to heal all that is preventing the love from being experienced within the hearts and souls of all humanity. The Goddess, as the great and beautiful Being that she is, is now to be honoured.

When you made the decision to come into this lifetime and take the responsibility of what a physical body represented, the greatest responsibility was to enable humanity to respond to Goddess and receive Her love. So we ask you to make clear that it is your responsibility to respond to the gift that is Goddess. As she gives you her great love and wisdom, it is your task and destiny to respond to that gift by being the willing receiver. Receiving her gift with gratitude and grace will facilitate the transformation of a humanity that is now ready and poised to step into the grandness of a plan now unfolding so powerfully and beautifully.

Cetaceans and Sirius

Many millions of years ago, when your planet was still very young, there was the first insurgence of the dolphins' and whales' energy from Sirius to find a dwelling place that would be in harmony with the vibration of their home planet. We wish you to understand here that Sirius A and B are suns and were suns at the time of which we speak. They are not planets. The planets revolve around these two suns.

When we talk about the Beings who came from Sirius, they came from the planets. The dolphins who came to Earth came from the planets revolving around Sirius. They dwelt on a system that had a vibration vastly different from your world now.

About 5,000 to 6,000 years ago, after your planet had fallen to its third-dimensional expression, it was deemed necessary for those beings to return again to your system called Earth. They returned to become the teachers to a humanity that had been thrown back into its primitive state yet again. These beings from Sirius had dwelt periodically upon your planet for many hundreds of thousands of years, taking different forms according to the cycles of Earth at that time. It is not necessary to describe all of those forms, but only to state that the beings from Sirius participated at specific places around your planet - Mesopotamia, Sumeria, South America and also in Africa and parts of India. These civilisations have historical records of visitors who have come from the stars and each has its legends of the Fish Gods. Those Beings from Sirius brought with them specific teachings, specific rituals and ceremony that provided keys that would facilitate an awakening consciousness to find the way home. It was seen as important and necessary that those who became the teachers, who came from the stars of Sirius, would teach ritual and ceremony that would be in harmony with the movement of the planets, the movement of the solar system in the galaxy, and the movement of the galaxy in relationship to the Universe.

These rituals and ceremonies activated consciousness and maintained brain patterns that were necessary for the evolution of consciousness. Equally, throughout your planet there were visitors from the Pleiades, visitors from other systems in your solar system. Each of the Gods throughout the Egyptian kingdoms represents an aspect of the consciousness of humanity and the Gods represent the characteristics and the qualities that each individual person would need to resolve and understand within himself.

We are only giving a small portion of the complexity. There are many who have been taking on physical form for many hundreds of thousands of years who had their origin with Sirius. Many of those who had been in physical form have no longer needed to continue. They now express themselves in their enlightened form and are now the composite of Sirius, sometimes blended with Pleiades, sometimes with Hathor and sometimes a combination of two with Annunaki.

Chapter IX
The Power Of Magic

Techniques

The Principles Of Alchemy

Ceremony And Ritual

The Chakras

The Power Of Kundalini

Meditation

Spirituality

CHAPTER NINE

The Power Of Magic

We wish to speak to you of magic; not the magic of the stage where rabbits are pulled from hats. The magic of which we speak is far more profound than any which you would see performed on stage.

We will speak of low magic and high magic. Magic uses the energies and vibrations which have their origin in the higher dimensions and which lie beyond time and space; yet operate according to divine law. When you learn the principle of divine law then you will create miracles of change and transformation within your own life.

Your understanding of the tools of magic will serve you well as you obey the laws and always work in harmony with the foundational principles. In this way you will set yourself free from bondage and limitation and move from darkness into light.

We will remind you of a principle which is known to you all, but we will explain it in a way that will provide a deeper understanding. In your world there is force and form. These are the main players in creation and destruction, life and death. They also provide the momentum for you to move from one dimension to another. All of creation from the original Source began as force. As it stepped down from the higher dimension it became increasingly trapped in form.

When opposing forces meet they will either attract or repel each other, ultimately creating a spinning ring which descends to a lower plane. Form is simply force which has locked itself up in patterns of its own making. In a similar way when a form is broken the force is released and becomes free-moving energy which will then move to a higher plane. Said in a different way, a form is built by interlocking the higher forces to create a form on a lower level. When the form is broken, the forces return to their original higher level. This principle is at work in everything you create. We will give you an example. If you seek to make a cake you will take the ingredients necessary, apply a force and bind them into a form. The cake is eaten and its form is broken down into its constituents and the energy released provides the body with nourishment. In a similar way you have also created your own beliefs. We will illustrate. As a child, the force may have been your father's wrath. You created a set of interpretations and locked the force into a belief that may have been 'men are to be feared'. In order to set yourself free you will need to use the magic of your mind to break down the old pattern and release the energy. That will then ultimately enable you to move to a higher level of expression.

Low magic provides a technique or set of steps within a ritual or ceremony to enable old patterns to be changed or broken down so the energy to be released can lift you into higher dimensions. The techniques are performed with full conscious awareness. In past times, ritual and ceremony were performed within all native cultures. The churches and temples performed ritual and ceremony with the explicit purpose of lifting consciousness from one level of expression to another. Specific words of power would be used to break old mind sets and encourage the integration of new patterns of thinking. As you will see, all change is the result of breaking down the old and creating the new, on either a higher or lower level. One releases energy to facilitate the movement to a higher level of expression; the other binds energy to take it down to a lower level of expression.

You as a humanity have been binding your power to form for hundreds of thousands of years. You have bound yourself to a set of beliefs which limit and constrain you in all areas of your life so that the only escape you have is death. Death is the grandest example of the process of breaking down old patterns. Every part of the physical body is broken down and returns to its original source. The task that is before you now invites you to begin to break down the old patterns and release the force in a conscious way so you can move consciously into the higher dimensions and so return to your higher source.

Many of you are afraid of the potency of the forces which you are aware are locked up within you. You may begin step by step. *It is preferable to be in control of your own transformation rather than have the forces of nature pushing the issue.* That is the challenge for you at this time. Your world is changing and all of the old structures are being broken down. It is for you the individual to facilitate that change as you move into the greater and the grander expression of your true self.

At this point we will not discuss techniques of high magic. It is only necessary that you understand the movement from low magic into high magic is a gradual process which only takes place when you as the individual have a complete grasp of the principles involved in low magic. High magic takes place in the deeper levels of your mind, within your own subconscious and unconscious. High magic facilitates an ease of transformation and enables change to take place miraculously. With high magic you work with ease using the higher dimensional energies.

Techniques

The purpose of low magic is to provide techniques which will assist you in your own personal transformation. As you live in a holographic world, applying techniques to yourself will also impact on your outer world. You may divide your life into specific areas and approach each in an organised way. For example, we would recommend each of you look at your physical health, your emotional health, your relationships, your career path and your financial status to begin with. Your task is to discover the beliefs you have established around each of these, for example:, you may have made the decision at a young age that sickness provided you with attention and love. That pattern continues into your adult life. There are many books to assist you to discover the symbolic meaning behind many of your illnesses. We suggest you take advantage of these. Your purpose is to break the old patterns to enable your body to be healed.

In addition to discovering the beliefs you have about your body, you will also need to discover what you believe about expressing yourself emotionally. Each of you has made decisions early in life and has either decided to be a thinker or a feeler. The other was deemed either inappropriate or too difficult. Conditioning from childhood may have influenced you to believe that crying was unacceptable, anger was definitely not tolerated and if you were to be socially acceptable, you must repress all of your emotions and pretend that everything is fine.

We say that *any emotion that is not appropriately expressed is negative.* This also includes love. There are many who are afraid of love and certainly do not know how to express it. When you find emotions coming to the surface, it is most important that you acknowledge them and recognise their value. Emotions are the force which enable you to move into a higher expression of yourself. Even anger, when expressed appropriately, without blame and with full responsibility, enables a strengthening of self-esteem and self-regard.

When you assess your relationships, it is most important to become aware of all of your relationships, including your boss, the next-door neighbour who is causing conflict with your family, your best friend who is always there for you, the other 'friends' who drain you, your most intimate partner and also your relationship to your parents, even if they have already made their transition in one form or another.

Your relationship with those around you will reveal much about you and your relationship to yourself. Perhaps you are protective, defensive or fearful, feel used, dominated, not listened to, not cared about, not important, not recognised or not valued. It is for you to listen to yourself talk and determine the way you describe each situation. This will reveal the beliefs you carry with you which need to be changed to release the energy surrounding them.

In a similar way it is important to discover what value you place on money. Many on the spiritual path see money and material possessions as unacceptable and many remain poverty-stricken because they have not seen how much power they give to it. In your world of illusion you may have as little of it or as much of it as you believe you can have. Remember, you have entered the universe to discover how to create. Many of you put unnecessary weight on money. It is simply an energy to be used so that you may discover your potential to express more of yourself in as many ways as possible. Indeed money and material possessions in general may indicate how willing you are to receive. *Your task is to learn how to receive love.* If your financial balance is in the red it will generally indicate you have very little value for yourself and the abilities you have lying dormant within you and also how willing you are to love yourself enough to trust yourself. Remember, you create your own reality. If you are not happy with any part of it, you can create it differently.

The principles of alchemy

In times gone by, alchemists were by tradition initiates of a high degree. To protect themselves and their secret wisdom they clothed the information in a set of symbols. They spoke of turning a base metal into gold and there were many who sought the illusive technique to create this valuable metal. The secret lay within the symbol, for this was a method of transformation of the basic human soul into its transcendent Self. The purification of the soul and its ultimate union with the eternal enabled death to be transcended.

There were four degrees of initiation in the process of transformation. These were designated as Fire, Water, Air and Earth. The initiation of Fire is the transmutation of desire. It enables the initiate to control the body functions including those of the internal organs. The Water initiation enables control of the emotions and of the psychic body and mind. The veils between the dimensions disappear and the initiate is no longer constrained by space. The initiation of Air bestows the power of becoming invisible at will. It enables the initiate to transcend the body and travel in the astral realms. The Earth initiation enables the ability to change the course of nature. By the act of willing it is possible for the initiate to place himself anywhere on the Earth or beyond it. These initiations can be experienced by those of you here who have the desire to apply themselves to the task at hand. A great number have indeed already taken many of the necessary steps toward that end in previous life experiences. This will facilitate an ease of continuing your own development in your present life. The necessary steps are very evident for the would-be seeker after 'gold'. Dedication and commitment are very necessary qualities needed by each person. You will require an understanding of the elements and how they function in your personal lives in relationship to your action, your body, emotions, your thinking and your spiritual Self

Ceremony and ritual

All ceremony and ritual is performed with an understanding of the four elements of fire, water, air and earth; the four directions of south, west, east, and north; and the ways in which the angelic hierarchy may be invoked to assist in the transformational and alchemical process to change the base nature into its transcendent Self (gold).

We advise each individual who has a mind to become Christed to set aside the time to connect with these elements both in nature and within Self. Your physical temple can be as elaborate or simple as you feel comfortable. You may even use the living room of your home after you have set aside the mundane furniture and cleansed the area that you are to use. The space may be returned to its original use after you have performed the necessary ceremony. Your particular ceremony will always need to be dedicated to a specific purpose. As you have in mind personal transformation you may wish to systematically go through each of the four elements one by one over a period of a month, with a week for each element. During a particular week you will focus on the associations for an element and work towards mastery (not control) of the element within yourself. In this way, over time, you will successfully heal Self of all the dross that contaminates the pure Self. Do be patient with yourself and always call upon your higher Self to be with you in all that you do.

Those beings who have been called to be present in the sacred space may then assist you to journey forth into the realms beyond so you may become familiar with the inter-dimensional spaces beyond time and space. You may also create for yourselves in that inner space the opportunities whereby those who are the great teachers, may join with you, enter into that sacred space and there hold counsel together. In the sharing of wisdom all will be the beneficiaries. There, in that sacred space, there is the opportunity for great light and great love to pour down.

In such a ritual, at the New Moon, the Full Moon and the times of solstice and equinox and the times of the special celebrations of Goddess, there will be a renewing of the power and the principle of the relationship to all of creation and an understanding that there is no separation of man and woman, the planet and all her expressions, and the ultimate of All-That-Is. Within the individual there will be an awakening of the grand expression of the universal order. Remember, you have come into this lifetime to be as Christ beings. Allow yourselves to be magicians, miracle-makers and the ones who would draw upon the counsel of Elders, those who have their being beyond the mists of time and who are able to access the timeless and bring it into the illusion of time.

You are here to become Masters. You are here to gain mastery over the limitations of an illusion in a world full of limitation. You are here to utilise the principles of spiritual law, to understand those principles and give expression to them and to learn how all things are created. In your active exploration of how the principles of creation function, thus you will fine-tune, and you will no longer need the ritual and ceremony. You will enable yourself to create through the power of thought, through the power of image.

The chakras

Through a deeper understanding of the principles which govern the functioning of the body - physical, emotional, psycho-spiritual and etheric - each individual can facilitate the transformation with greater ease. These functions connect to similar patterns of energy through planet Earth and the cosmic dance, which harmonises and draws humanity and the solar system into the dance of a pattern laid down aeons of light years ago. Your physical bodies are the microcosm within the macrocosmic universe. As you understand Self, so will you understand All-That-Is.

The planetary and stellar configurations are all changing position in specific ways at this time. As there are stars in the heavens, so there are cells in the brain and body of the individual. The way the stars interact with each other creates specific activations which enable the release of information that will also activate the brain cells and pathways in the individual. The body has within it those vital doorways, each of the major chakras in the body. There are twelve which equate to the twelve constellations. Each of the twelve chakras will have its association with the constellations of the zodiac. Each is a doorway unto the other.

The interplay between the body and the stellar configurations will be significant in the times ahead, because the stellar configurations are now changing in specific ways. By their very nature, they influence the chakras, which are in themselves stellar configurations within the body. The chakras are now changing in quite dramatic ways. They function on the twelve levels within the body and the twelve levels through the twelve dimensional gateways beyond the body. In their combinations, they are equivalent to twelve by twelve - the 144 computations of varying interactions amongst each.

Each person may find the inflow of energies through the gateways will impact in different ways according to where there are still blocks within the body related to the gateways. It is now imperative, more than ever before, for each person intending to participate consciously in the transformational journey, to spend some time in meditation and solitude to activate the gateways to receive the stellar inflow.

Each of the chakras, as it is activated, will flow according to the spiralling patterns laid down even before the physical Earth came into expression. These spiralling energies are reproduced and recreated in ways and patterns which are identical to the movement of the cosmic dance of the whole of the universal galaxies. The chakras correlate to the cosmic dance, yet you as a humanity have encased yourself in a protective shell and have not been able to receive the cosmic inflow for quite some time. This is now changing.

There was a period of time, several thousand years before your Christ being entered your world, when a temple called the Temple Of Solomon was established. There were gateways in the temple, which existed on three dimensions. In all there were twelve gates, one to the north, south, east and west - each on three dimensional expressions - to create the twelve gateways. In a similar manner, you as individuals have your own gateways that relate to the four foundational principles - fire, air, water and earth. Each of these has its four modes of expression, the spiritual, mental, emotional and physical. An alchemical process will begin when you as an individual consciously apply the principles of elemental energy in a specific way. You will create balance and harmony to allow the four principles to be the foundation stone, the platform upon which is built the immortal body of the Christ light.

Question: Can you describe the significance of the chakras in our spiritual journey?

Our preference is to refer to these vortices as gateways, so as not to confuse them with the traditional chakra system. There are those that exist within the physical body and those that extend beyond it.

The first of the twelve is the foundational chakra and it is found at the perineum. Within that gateway can be found the original blueprint or genetic code which holds the resonance of the individual person to his purpose and destiny. This is aligned to the great work and the purpose for the first creative impulse. It is here you will find the element of fire and the passion for life. The force from this centre enables the pattern or form to take shape in the foetus. The form is demonstrated in the sacrum which is the solid physical structure representing *the second chakra*. This centre also has its relationship to the hands and the feet. This centre represents your willingness to be physical and to feel safe in a physical world. This relates to your willingness to handle the circumstances of your life and walk your path, your purpose and destiny and the reason why you were born.

The third gateway was activated during the time of the separation of the sexes, that of male and female. Prior to that time the human form was androgynous and whole; male and female in one. The third centre represents also historically that period of time when the moon began to influence the developing human form. The physical organs represented by this gate are the sexual organs in all of the kingdoms of nature. All of nature requires the interaction of both the sun and the moon for conception and creation to take place in the physical world.

This gateway provides the principles for relationships and creation. All creative processes require both a male energy and a female energy. The male energy represents the spirit/mind and thought, and the female provides the soul/heart and intuition. Within each person, an open and receptive heart receives the seed of spirit and intuition and responds with creative action to form a new life or physical form. By expressing your own heart's desire, creating what excites you the most, you will always be in harmony with your purpose and destiny.

The fourth gateway is positioned at your solar plexus. It is the gateway through which flow all of the experiences that you have come to karmically transform and heal. On the grand scale, as we take you back into your far distant past, you find your connections to those who came from distant planets and who interfered with your original purpose; many who caused major changes within the human form and created a massive fear within the human psyche. This gateway stores many of your beliefs and emotions which block you from fulfilling your destiny. Your emotional karma from many lifetimes blocks access to the energy behind this gateway. Your present life will provide all that you require to heal the past. While you give power to some external event as preventing you from doing something you would like to do, realise your response comes from an old *fear of the consequence* of doing what you love to do. It is time to change that. Secret Governments, men in black, ghosts, the law, your boss, black magic, all represent the principle of loss of your personal power to express yourself. You are here in this life to learn not to give your power away. *Nothing can harm you except the belief that it will.*

The next two gateways are close together. They create the divisions between conditional and unconditional love. The conditional love relates to the thymus gland and to that period of time when there was the need to protect and defend against the threat to life. During that time, choice was between attacking and defending or feeling powerless and intimidated. The immune system is the physical organ that responds to those old messages. It maintains its old stance of defence and protection against the threat to life. In your external world you have created defence systems, boundaries between countries and weapons of war. There will come a time when these are no longer needed.

Next to the thymus is the gateway to love. Here is the beginning of a love that concerns love of a close, or significant, person and those who are in harmony with Self. In the opening of the following gates the love expands into love of humanity, through to universal love at the twelfth gate. At this gate there is love without fear or condition. Here is the chalice, the meeting place of the Divine Spirit within the human. Here is the cauldron where it is possible to create the elixir of life that can nourish the body and the multitudes. As one loves unconditionally, the sacred chalice releases a tone through the seven layers of muscle in the heart, causing every cell to resonate harmonically. This tone is intercepted by the thymus gland which in turn releases a chemical that heals the physical body and the soul. Love of Self is as important as love for another.

As we move to the thyroid gland we come to the *seventh gate.* At this gate the Holy Logos finds its expression in form. Each word that ushers forth from your mouth can reveal its source. They may be words from the lower worlds or they may express the sacred wisdom from the higher realms. Those who would speak from their heart and the divine source will speak words that delight the soul and lift the spirit to great heights.

The pituitary and pineal centres are gateways to the higher realms. Herein you will find access to spiritual senses that enable you to listen to the voices of the inner worlds and to see with your spiritual eyes. As each individual awakens to the highest principle and aligns with his higher Self, he will begin to function in the outer world in such manner as to be of total service to humanity. There are also two further gateways above the head, and another below the feet. Remember that each of the gateways is a hologram of all of the other gateways. Each connects to all of the others and so it is possible to reach the highest through the lowest. The gateways above the head will enable access to the energies of the galactic and universal sources. It is inappropriate to assign each of the gateways to a specific dimension because each is connected to all dimensions. The centre below the feet anchors each to the consciousness or soul of the Earth. Each of those gateways will have its own gatekeeper. They belong to the angelic and archangelic realms. They in turn have their allegiance to the guiding principles of the celestial zodiac and the greater cosmic principles.

By opening the gates on all levels and clearing the energies blocking the flow of energy through you, you will draw to yourself the ruling principle or gatekeeper that is connected to each of those gateways. The gatekeepers will then lead you along those pathways that are as celestial maps in the multidimensional universe. Every cell in your body has a consciousness and every consciousness has a guiding influence. Every blade of grass has an elemental being to assist it in its growth and development. None develop without support and encouragement. All are guided into the fullness of their expression in harmony with the principles of the Divine.

Even the baby at the first stages of conception has those who hover around to monitor the ways in which the cells divide and form the body and the organs. Each stage of growth is monitored by angelic beings who maintain the principles of creation and regeneration.

The power of the kundalini

There is a fire that burns deep within. There is a fire that is the animating principle that enables each person to be conscious. The kundalini functions on many levels. Without it you would surely die.

It is what animates the life of the body. It is the principle of warmth. It is also the principle of coolness, depending on how it flows.

The kundalini energy flows through the meridians of the body, yet it also functions on an even higher dimensional level within the psyche of each individual, for it is also that principle that, when united with the light of love of the heart, enables the individual to have eternal life. When this principle flows into the higher realms of consciousness, it provides the means for each chakra to be awakened to its potential to function on the astral and spiritual realms. The kundalini force, when it flows appropriately, activates the endocrine glands, enabling them to give health and vitality to the physical body.

It also enables the higher centres to perform the ultimate function such that the individual person who has become Christed will be able to perform miracles of healing, will have access to the source of all wisdom and will love unconditionally. Many gifts are attributed to the kundalini as it rises and activates the chakra system. When the kundalini rises in its fullness, then the individual is immortalised and spiritualised.

Meditation

In the Mystery schools of old you learned many truths, and one of those was to sit in meditation. Meditation is essential to the discovery of yourself. Your relationship with your Self is of primary importance. Many avoid relating to themselves by making themselves busy, constantly creating diversions. You decide there are many other important tasks to be done, except being willing to sit with yourself, to explore yourself and to become intimate with yourself.

Oh! But you do love to become intimate with others, yes? "I must go and visit my friend, talk to them on the telephone." "Got to know those favourite characters on my regular television program, must find out what they are doing next." But have you explored *yourself?* Have you sat in the stillness, the quietness, for the periods of time that you would give to your friends? Have you endeavoured to get to know yourself? You may be afraid you will not like yourself and of what

175

you might find. Yes, you may be afraid of what you might find. You might find yourself to be so profoundly powerful, so profoundly wise, with such capacity to love, that you frighten yourself with your abilities. You are here to discover that you are so very powerful! You are wise beyond measure. You have so much to give, and yet you are not giving to *yourself.*

As you sit in meditation, you will learn to communicate with yourself, with the highest principle within. As love is given and received, your knowledge will change. Although there may be upheavals in the land, those who hold fast to the spiritual principles will experience less trauma. It is most important that you spend time on a regular basis attuning and rebalancing your own electrical and magnetic fields by meditating to centre Self.

You might say you have no time. We suggest you either go to bed a little later, if night time is your best time, or to go to bed a little earlier if you find that morning is better. This is far more important on the greater scale than it is for you to stay in bed until perhaps 7.00 in the morning the time you would normally arise. It is more conducive to you to arise at 5.00 to 5.30 in the morning and in that period set aside your time when you may centre Self and prepare Self for the day ahead, for the week ahead, or for the year ahead.

Question: Is the activation of the chakra heightened during the meditation process and will that activation occur to all, whether they meditate or not?

Every single person on the planet is activated. This also means that all the chakras are activated. Those who meditate, and those who meditate specifically on the chakras, activate each chakra in accordance with its purpose. If there are blockages within some chakras for some people, these also will come to the surface both in the meditator and the non-meditator. Meditators have the advantage of facilitating the clearing with greater ease. The activation allows the harmonising of each chakra with the other. When there are blockages within the chakra, the blockages are magnified. It is a magnification process.

We also recommend practising creative visualisation. Practise imagination. Utilise all of your senses to create those spaces within meditation whereby you are able to smell, taste, touch and hear. Make it vivid so you are able to *feel* the touch of a feather, and *feel* what it is like to have talcum powder poured on to your hands. *Feel* the touch of water, and feel the difference between water that is cool and water that is warm. Let yourself become a tree. Let yourself move around the tree. Let yourself become a leaf on the tree. In this way you will be exercising the visualisation ability. This will assist you as you move more consciously on to the astral planes when you will use your astral senses, your clairvoyant and telepathic senses.

It is in the ability to meditate that you enable yourself to discover your own personal ability, your own wisdom and love, your own centre and creative ability. It is in the inner Self through meditation that you will be able to communicate with those of the inner planes, demonstrating for yourselves the ability to go beyond the limitations of the rational and the logical into the inspirational and the intuitive. Meditation, if performed with awareness, dedication and commitment, will open many doors and will empower you to live your life according to the destiny for which you have come in this life.

Remember, you are here in this life to have joy, to play with this substance you call matter, not to be trapped by it. You learn how to play with it in much the same way a child would play with clay. You are able to change its shape according to your desires. You consider this physical substance to be dense, almost immovable. In meditation, you can visualise the same shape, but you can bend it. Practise bending the shape, so it can become what you wish it to become in creative visualisation, in imagination. As you do that in meditation, it will form itself into its new creation in this world of matter.

Be aware that your physical body *is* your spiritual body stepped down. We will ask you to create this analogy: You have a rubber band. You stretch it, and stretch it, and stretch it, and a little bit out here finds its way into the Earth, the world. This bit out here is Spirit, this bit here is matter. It is still the same substance, is it not? Except that it has changed its vibration along the way. It is all made of the same one substance. There is nothing in the whole of creation that is not of the same one substance. There is not a different substance. Everything is made of the *one* substance. *All* of you is spiritual including this physical form. It is just Spirit manifesting in different ways. Is the ice block made of anything different than the water, the vapour, or the steam? Each is the same, except vibrating at a different rate. This is important for you to understand, for there are many who would denigrate the body by saying it is not spiritual. It is.

In the transitional time, old emotions will be shaken free and these may well be of sadness or grief. There may be overwhelming feelings of loneliness or incredible feelings of anger, rage and frustration. Whatever emotions still reside within the subconscious, which you have not as yet cleared, will be brought to the surface and will be experienced in very unusual ways, unmistakably spontaneous and almost as if you are not sure of where they came from! It is often happening that fast.

Equally, there will be others who will sense and feel the changes taking place within their own thinking. We say 'sense and feel' because your thinking is intimately connected with your feeling. The thoughts will become quite unusual in many ways because of their circular and analytical motion. You could find yourself going back into old patterns of mental behaviour, realising that what you thought to have stopped long ago is coming back again. The energies that are pouring into your planet now have the task of assisting you to change. And so you may well wonder why you are bringing up all of this old 'stuff'? The reason is very simple, so you may be rid of it! Many will also experience total mental breakdowns. You may hear about someone who has lost his mind. They cannot stop the overflow. Many will need assistance. Be aware it is because of the increased energy on your planet. You will then be able to take a step back and become the observer, taking possession of your life again by centring yourself.

In all of these changes, there is one thing that is required of you to allow those changes to take place with greater ease, and that is *to establish and re-establish your relationship with your idea of God/ Goddess.* This is the time when you begin to embrace that choice: "I will do my meditation and set aside the time." It is a time when you go to your centre and remain centred. Whenever you feel as if it is moving too fast, as if it is too much, it is time to sit and centre yourself and call upon the guides and counsellors of your higher Self. Begin each morning and end each day with a period of silence, a period of centring and a period of activation and cleansing of each of the chakras of your body. Fill them with light. Fill them with love.

This will be your way of nourishing the planet, allowing energy to flow into your particular area and to safeguard it from the possibility of earthquakes. Earthquakes can only occur when you are not utilising the electromagnetic energies being poured into your planet.

Spirituality

You are invited - in particular in this year of 1997 - to focus so very much more than you have ever done before on honouring yourself as the spiritual being that you are. Those who resist the spiritual aspects of the Self will go through a crisis, and we call it a crisis of spirituality which will be felt in your psychiatry, your psychology, your emotion- ality and genetic patterning. In your own unique ways you will find your life coming to somewhat of a crisis at this point, in varying degrees. Some will shrug their shoulders and feel it is just fine. Others will feel as if it is getting very close to the end of the road, with their backs against the wall and without any other choices left. We will bring in certain areas of discussion so you may understand the varying stages that you may experience. Your own decision to transcend the limitations of space/time and the desire to go home is the compelling force behind these changes, compelling many of you to become more involved in your spirituality.

Your world as you know it is changing. The consciousness of this planet has changed dramatically, even as recently as the beginning of this year. As a result, you need to lift that frequency to be in resonance with the soul of the planet. Those who feel out of synchronicity with the planet will need to make major decisions, and these decisions can be made in various areas such as relationships, career, finance and health and are to be made now. Each will face aspects of those decisions that will impact in the four areas named.

What is your psychiatry? It is that aspect of you that relates to the soul in relationship to your spirituality, in relationship to the narrow edge on which you walk that can throw you into insanity or into your spirituality. That line is so narrow. Those who are being called to their spirituality may refuse for varying reasons, based on previous life patterns that still exist and hold them in old patterns of conformities. These will need to be processed through so that you are free to reclaim your spirituality.

That narrow line is there, and facing you in the decisions you make: "Shall I continue in my expansion, in my relationship with All-That-Is and in that willingness, am I prepared to set aside a regular period that is devoted to soul-searching in order to know more about myself and my relationship with All-That-Is, God/Goddess?"

By making those decisions, you will claim and maintain your sanity, maintaining that part of your brain that allows the greater light to come through, rather than the insanity that creates the darkness and the confusion. It is the understanding of your emotionality from the perspective of your soul and that which represents the feminine principle or the Goddess energy that is within you. *Now*, the light of Goddess calls you forth to enable the balancing of the Spirit and the soul and to allow that relationship to unfold. Those who refuse to allow the healing of those aspects that are to do with the betrayal of the soul, the rejection and the denial of the soul's urge to give expression to itself, will face the crisis of their psychology, the crisis of that level of emotions that relates directly to the soul.

There will be a broadening of emotionality as it links with your relationship to yourself and to those experiences from your childhood. Know you are now being called to address the shadow self. You have created a very significant dynamic with the shadow that was born with you and trails behind you as your shadow does when you walk. If you did not see your shadow you would be a little concerned, would you not? Who was it who lost his shadow and had to have it sewn back on again? Peter Pan, yes! He needed his shadow. You all need your shadow. Your shadow is your friend. Your negative ego is not your friend. Now is the time to balance the books. Do not to push it into the bag that is carried by your shadow, but become whole again, allow the emotional being that you are to claim your real Self.

So many of you now will be facing circumstances concerning health, the dynamics of the workplace and those to whom you relate in the workplace. You will face your shadow in your personal and intimate relationships. Your shadow is seeking for you to know what has been pushed down and what is beneath the surface, in order for you to understand what you have available and to claim those beautiful, light and powerful qualities.

The American Indians had a medicine bag containing the magical tools and instruments, which enabled them to perform the magic that created the miracles of their life. You have the magic bag also! Your magic bag contains your instruments of magic. In this year of your time, you, all of you, are going to face the crisis in some area of your life. That crisis will be there so you can say: "What tools do I have available in my medicine bag, to enable me to perform the miracles of transformation, to draw upon the positive I have within me?"

We have said you will face your crises: crises of different kinds, different shapes, different forms. The message is to encourage you to access the shadow side, that part of you which you have denied. As you change your own psychology, your emotionality and the beliefs that have been imprinted, stored in the many nooks and crannies of your DNA, so will those blueprints change. You are here in this lifetime to facilitate the greatest change of all time. *The crisis of your spirituality is the crisis of your refusal to change.*

This year an avalanche of opportunities is given to you, opportunities that seem to come from everywhere. It will seem as if you could do this, or that, and this and also that as well! "What am I going to do?

It is too much. I think I will go to bed instead." It is as if, in the inundations of opportunities, you decide to close the door and hibernate. It is that decision that creates the crisis of your spirituality. It is your inability to accept the opportunities and move into them and allow them to be the source of change that will cause your trauma. You are now called to the task, that you now *live* your spirituality in every breath you breathe, in every footstep, in every motion and thought. You are, and always have been, totally spiritual, yet you live your lives as if you are human, and you are now asked to change your identity. You are spiritualising your idea of who you are, and those who continue to maintain 'I am human' will find that this determination will create their crises.

Within the higher dimensional aspect of yourself, you have made a decision that haste is in order. You are moving forward very quickly and as a result you are creating wonderful opportunities, even the opportunity to make your dream come true. Oh, it is *that* far away... so close - that dream you always dreamed, that you wanted for yourself! You are about to embrace it, and that you *could* embrace it fills you with fear. Your life *could* work so very beautifully and powerfully!

"Oh, can I handle such a beautiful, successful, happy lifetime? Oh no, I am not ready for that yet. I still want to punish myself, deny myself, become a bit more of the victim and go into my self-pity, maintaining the old stances a little bit longer, perhaps." It is then that the crises of your spirituality will tap you on the shoulder and say "Come, come out of the closet. Here is what you are waiting for! This is what you have always wanted", smiling at you, beckoning you. "Destiny is calling. Opportunities await you."

Without exception, all of you are encouraged to claim your spiritual Self, to live it completely; to be able to say to yourself with full knowledge: " I Am That I Am. I am that light and that love. I have the wisdom within me that I can call upon." Oh yes, you all do. It is not that you do not at times search for other avenues, for the spiritual Self knows that if you need to find certain information you may go to your municipal library. Those who seek to find information about the stars can go to an astronomer. Those who seek to know about the weather can seek out the weather man. You have created avenues of information on multiple levels, and one such level is your third-dimensional world which is a very rich source of information that you do not need to deny to yourself. Yet there is a very profound knowledge and a wisdom that can be accessed as you claim your spirituality, a wisdom that can be yours when you become at one with your higher Self and you are then able with great conviction to say: "I am That I Am."

Let your radiance shine. See the indicators that you are not whole and complete and allow the integration to take place. The solutions for your healing are available to you from so many sources. It is not a time to become emotionally crippled, to face death in the varying degrees: physical, emotional, mental or spiritual. It is time to claim your Life - all of it! *There is so much excitement awaiting you.*

For so very long you have had various ideas and interpretations about spirituality. Many of you have gone through traditional Sunday schools and learned about God and the church, and about Mary and Jesus, and you learned to behave yourselves on that one day of the week, did you not? You dressed in your finest clothing, and you sat rigid and still, without smiling and pretending to be so very pious, yes? And then, at the end of the day, you relaxed and you loosened your constraints, and you decided that it was time you could have some fun again.

Spirituality was, at that time, not having enjoyment. Spirituality was confining, it was demanding, it was so very serious, was it not? It forced you into a particular mould, for what you could or should do, or what you could or should not do, in the expression of yourself and the degree to which you were able to do or not do. You found yourself interpreted as a saint or a sinner and you had carried with you the burden of the ancient sin, still held so very firmly in place in your heart and your soul. It is held so firmly in fact, that it is only this year that many of you will shed the remnants of guilt and shame, the remnants of sin - a sin that many of you do not remember.

We would like to assist you to reclaim more of what spirituality was meant to be in your life and to embrace more of that in the joyfulness of your freedom and expression. This is the period of awakening of the spirituality that has never been experienced quite like this before.

You have known, we are sure, that you are forerunners. You have known and you do know that this is such a crucial time for you, as mapmakers, pathfinders and creators of the new destiny.

You have learnt, and are still learning, how to be creators of a new kind and how to empower yourselves as male and female, different from what has been before. Now you stretch even further and claim and reclaim a spirituality that is unlike any before. You are to create a *new* type of spirituality and you may ask the question "How do we know what to create?" Well, we say, you have now come of age, realising the fullness of the being that you are, created in the image of God. Your Bible says explicitly that Adam was created in the image of God. Adam was not a man, in the idea of what you would consider man to be. Adam was quite unique, the first prototype, and as such was not physical in the way you understand physical. Adam was created in the image of God, having the totality of All-That-Is within the vastness of that first being and, out of that one, came the two, the division and the separation into duality or polarity. Out of Adam, or the ONE, came Eve the DUALITY, not as the rib as you have been taught in Sunday school, but rather as the Soul. Where the female contained the male and the male contained the female, there was then a stepping down, and so we relay again to you what was meant to be in your Holy Book, 'created in the image', as was imagined, so it is created.

And now creativity and imagination have come of age. You will understand that your spirituality is relying on your creativity and your imagination. For years, your spirituality has been confounded by the many so-called religious ideas. For example, you have been told that to be truly spiritual you must be vegetarian, and, if you are not vegetarian, how can you possibly be spiritual? You have also been

184

told that spiritual people are to live in poverty; that if you are truly spiritual you could not possibly live in a mansion and drive a luxurious car. Spiritual people are poor people. Poor. Poor in body, rich in spirit. This is a concept that has been engendered by the Church, so the Church can have the money; and so you feel good about handing it over to your Church.

We hasten to say that spirituality is not dependent on how much you do not have by way of your physical resources, it is rather the measure of your perception of yourself. Your spirituality encompasses all of your life. We have heard people who tend to somehow isolate their lives and say: "One day I will become spiritual. I will devote an hour every day to my meditation, and that will make me spiritual. I will say my prayers during that time, and that will also help me to become spiritual." We again hasten to say that we cannot make you any more spiritual than you already are. You have never been separated from All-That-Is. There never was a separation, except in your own mind. You have always been and always will be One with All-That-Is. You cannot isolate your spirituality to a portion of your day and say in that particular time slot you will be spiritual. The very cells of your body are made of God. Everything is of God. *There is nothing that is not of God*, and so, to you who resent your physicality and who say: "One day I will leave my body and I will go home", we say this *is* your home. Your body is the temple of the living light. You are made of light! You are made of God.

Your scientists are now realising, as they take the molecules of your body down to the very elements, the atoms and the subatomic particles, and down into the protons and the neutrons and the neutrinos and various other subatomic particles, down to the very energy itself, that the basic substance behind everything is light. The very cells of your body have as their foundation particles of light.

We tell you that you are spiritual beings, beings of light, that there is not one cell in your body that is not of light. Therefore, each moment of your day then becomes an expression of your spirituality. What is your purpose in life? To realise that you are of light.

This subject of spirituality is one you will need to explore in greater depth. We remind you that you are creators of a new form of spirituality. You see, you have been functioning very much under the limitations of linear thinking. As you open up your mind to the greater spiritual dimensions, you will find that the creator in you will bring forth from above rather than from your third dimension. You will live your life through your spirituality. Every part of your life will be expressed as you, the spirit.

Chapter X
New Technologies

Economy And Money
Knowledge Becomes Power
Technologies
Work

CHAPTER TEN

New Technologies

Economy and money

You are spiritual beings who have come into this universe in order to enjoy creating out of the very substances which are available to you. Indeed you are doing just that, except you have lost sight of the joy and are now so engrossed in the illusion that you have allowed it to control you and to be your god. There are two dynamics we wish you to explore in your minds. One is a very positive and affirming dynamic and it is through this that we and many others of our kind wish to congratulate you. You have gone into the depths of illusion or physical matter and have become masters in learning how to shape it, bend it and mould it into everything you are able to see in your world. You have created vast technologies in all areas of life including physical, social, health, scientific, educational and political areas.

You have overcome gravity to such a degree you are able to send spacecraft to the other side of your solar system. You have learned to cultivate the land, forge the metal and communicate via satellites through many devices so that every home is a communication relay station. You have learned well and have indeed mastered matter beyond what was originally intended.

Now you are approaching your final test. You are now facing the challenge to transform matter back to its original form. This will require an understanding of physics and chemistry which goes beyond your modern laboratories. It is the understanding of how patterns and structures in one dimension or level hold the energy that will enable the movement to the next level of expression. In the process, the debris of the original level is left behind. You will understand this in relation to the process of eating food. The food you eat is bound together in a specific form. When it is taken into your body it is broken down. The energy which is released is absorbed into the cells of your body and the waste is discarded. This is a very crude way of describing an alchemical process.

There is a second dynamic we now wish to discuss with you. Having learned how to master matter, you have locked yourself into a paradigm of beliefs which restricts you to your third-dimensional expression. You are imprisoned by the scientific, social and political models you have created and are unable to see beyond them. The principles of alchemy exist on all levels and so we now desire to share with you ways in which you may use these principles to break down the old paradigm and move into the greater expression. Change or movement from one dimension to another requires breaking down old structures, releasing the energy contained within them and using that energy as the momentum to move to the next level.

A simple analogy is as follows. A person may have a set of beliefs that holds him in a particular job. This may be a belief of not feeling good enough to do anything beyond that. When the belief is changed a huge amount of energy is released to enable the person to assume a new status of expression. The same principle can be applied to change belief structures within education, health, social constraints, religious beliefs and many others. With the influence of the Aquarian Age and the inflow of the energy of the Goddess through the Sirius vortex, the old structures are broken down and huge volumes of energy are released. The energy is available to find new structures on a higher dimensional level. In this way you will be guided into the next millennium, creating and establishing new forms and structures on increasingly higher levels until you move through the veil of illusion and set yourself free of the constraints of time and space.

Knowledge becomes power

In an equal measure, the financial climate of your world will also shift and change. Your whole world will go through a financial adjustment where the base of power will no longer be determined by

190

those who have the greatest material assets. The acquisition of commodities will begin to have a different meaning.

Power will not be seen as how much money you have. Power will be seen as how much information you have, how much access you have to the information technologies, the computers and the media. Those who have the greatest degree of control over the information technology will be seen to have the most power.

The stock exchange will be unpredictable. This will be a reflection of changing values. Many of you are deciding information is more important than a new car every year. You are also realising the value of your environment, your health and the social situation that will begin to emerge as a major concern. You are now moving more fully into the Aquarian Age where mind, information and consciousness are expanding. Those countries which were seen in the past as financially successful will now be seen in a different light. Such countries as Japan, which have been seen to hold the balance through their financial success, will suddenly be faced with environmental and social crises which will change their stance and values.

There will certainly be changes in Europe where the economic fluctuations will cause instability and traumas for many. You (Australia) have been cushioned from much of the suffering which is taking place in such countries as Germany, Russia and China. While you have received a certain amount of information about war-torn countries, those who are not at war will soon be seen to experience total human degradation. A crisis point will be reached which will demand solutions. The world conscience will be activated. New solutions will begin to emerge.

You will see powerful people rising up to take responsibility for finding the solutions which will benefit all people. There will begin to emerge the real concept of a global community. You will realise, when any part of your world is in trauma or conflict, it affects the entire world. When you understand this in relationship to your own body you will see the impact this will eventually have. If you have a diseased liver or an infection in your lungs, those portions of your body are not separated from the rest of your body. In a similar way, those who have sufficient awareness will begin to realise the same principles apply to your world. When any part of your world is 'diseased' then it affects the entire world. While there are starving and homeless people, you will never find your way home. Until responsibility is taken to heal on all levels, then you as a humanity will not have come of age. You will realise it is no longer viable to have any one country deficit in any area, whether through financial or political upheaval. Knowledge and how to apply it will be necessary in a changing world.

Many may wait for the extraterrestrials in their flying machines to come and rescue them. We suggest it would be rather irresponsible to rescue anyone who did not understand the basic principles of transformation. After all, that is the reason you have entered into this life time. It would not be advisable to let you loose on another world. You just may destroy it in the same way you have been destroying your present world. Your task is to find the solutions. You have been creating and discarding your bodies for hundreds of thousands of years. You think you can do the same thing with worlds. In fact you have done just that in many cases. You have succeeded in destroying whole planets in the past. Now you have decided this lifetime will be different from all of the rest. You are no longer going to destroy and discard. *This time you will transform and transcend.*

There are many in your world who seek to sabotage and conspire against you who have decided that this is the lifetime to ascend. They still wish to maintain an old pattern of power through control and domination. They seek to continue wars and battles and in many cases, when peace is close at hand, they sabotage the process. They will not succeed, for the power of love and light from God/Goddess now works with you and for you. You will succeed beautifully, even though at times it may appear as if everything is against you, as if you will fall down into the mire of the quicksand that drags you under. Each time this appears to happen there will be the hand that will reach in and pull you out to enable you again to set forth.

Question: What will be of value rather than the almighty dollar? What will take its place?

The simple answer is *you*. As a humanity you are to be valued above and beyond any material possessions and ultimately beyond the power hungry who seek to keep you suppressed and powerless. You will begin to see evidence throughout your world of the ordinary person taking up his power. You will see it in small groups and indeed whole populations of people, who decide they no longer need to be at the mercy of a dominating leadership that does not serve them.

Each of you in your own way will find a new value system coming into your personal lives. Communication and communication devices will gain greater and greater importance in the future. This is very much in harmony with the Aquarian Age and the influence of Uranus and ultimately Neptune in Aquarius. Neptune with assistance from Pluto in Sagittarius, will activate all levels of communication right through to the higher dimensions of spirituality. Even in the market place, in the business sector and in politics, spirituality will be seen to be of major importance if success in any endeavour is to be achieved.

Those of you who have become aware will realise personal value is dependent on access to resources. These include your ability to access the higher levels of wisdom gained through your relationship with your higher Self. There will be an explosion of information greater than anything that has ever occurred so far. This explosion threatens to blow the circuits of your Internet. Information will be the growth industry for the new age. In all areas of your society, from the arts and education through to health and economics, new innovative ideas will emerge, with new ways to create solutions for old problems. Information will also be available in the areas of your own personal, metaphysical and spiritual growth. Information itself will be going through its own metamorphosis.

In expressing and extending yourselves in your own particular field, you will be asking: "How can I express myself more creatively, more productively? In what ways can I be of more benefit? What do I need to know? How can I access that greater resource of knowledge?" Those who are out there in the world who would never ever come to a place such as this are saying: "How can we resolve this trauma? How can we resolve this problem of not having enough food? How can we resolve the problem of the toxic waste, the polluted oceans, the ozone depletion and the greenhouse effect? How can we gain more knowledge? The knowledge we had in the past does not work, will not work. We know that now. How can we gain the knowledge?" Each will go beyond himself to access the resources that will enable him to find the answers. And the answers will be unique. The answers will be inspirational, full of surprises, the very surprises which we have discussed with you. You will be astonished and amazed: "Where did I get this information from? How did I access the way to do this?" and yet there will be those solutions.

There will be major influences coming into your planet, beginning this year for short periods of time, and then moving in an abundant way next year and continuing for quite some considerable time. These are creative revolutionary energies. The opportunities will make the experimenter and the leader, and the one who has the desire to be a leading edge in his particular field, suddenly realise he found a solution where previously he thought there was no solution!

There will be major breakthroughs in the areas of science and technology, in music and art, breakthroughs of such a manner that those who thought they had heard music will hear music of a different quality. It will be music created by those people who have really begun to open up to the spheres beyond your Earth, to those sounds that are of a higher vibration. As each attunes to the higher levels he will bring those sounds through, sounds that will touch your soul like you have never been touched before. And there are those who will find the way to create all manner of art - dance, painting, sculpture. Each will find his own way to create what is new, inspirational and transformational. This is the time of the greater revolution whereby each person is urged to go beyond himself, for each of you is expanding and developing exponentially, faster than you have ever considered possible for you. Yes, change, rapid change.

So when you find yourself 'thrust out of the nest', out of the security of your past, into the unknown of what to do now, where to go next, it is for you then to say: "What are my skills? How can I build on those? How can I utilise the information which comes from beyond myself so I can find the way to be creative and productive, that will facilitate change in the individual person who comes to me?"

Without exception, all of you will have a unique task to do. In discovering your task you will be participating with many others such as yourselves in this whole transformation. We wish to excite you! We wish to inspire you in one of the most powerful, creative and productive periods of your life which you have entered into this year.

And yet, because there are still many who hold on to the old ways, to familiar blockages within the individual and in the greater global humanity, there will be incidences that appear to be quite tragic, quite traumatic to the individual, to the family, to the group, to the country and to the nation. These are purposeful. They usher in this totally new, revolutionary change. Right down to the cellular levels of your bodies you will feel and sense those changes taking place within you.

Technologies

Question: In leaning towards connecting with nature, and natural things, what is going to happen to our technology?

In many ways technology is beginning to prove to be beneficial to you and we see two possible future scenarios. We mention two, because at this point in time we have not yet seen that the decisions you have made have been concrete.

We have indicated as well that, in the periods of time beyond 800,000 to 100,000 years ago, you were very close to nature. You worked totally in harmony with nature. In that past, your technology was one which was used by the shaman, the priest and the magician in their understanding and application of the spiritual laws and the laws of nature. Their technology was the application of natural law. You have gone beyond natural law and applied the principles that exist only in a third-dimensional world of limitation.

These same technologies will, in the first instance, provide the means to move beyond that very same limitation. Up to this point in time, many of your technologies have proven to be detrimental in the long term. They cause the breakdown of much that has been seen as the degradation of your planet. In many ways it has caused much of the pollution of your rivers and oceans, the depletion of the ozone layer, the green house effect, toxic waste and the accumulation of huge volumes of rubbish which do not break down in the normal way.

While there are already revolutionary technologies in existence that can clean all of the toxic waste from your environment, it has been necessary for each individual to overcome the dominating influence of those who seek to control the new scientific discoveries. *Knowing about those who conspire against you is insufficient to bring about change.*

As you are ready to take up your power, there will be much excitement about many new revolutionary discoveries that will assist you to lift your world out of its self-destructive ways into new patterns of healing and transformation. Medical and environmental science, for example, will be two major areas where technology will prove to be of great benefit to humanity. The study of the human body and that of animals on the land and in the sea will provide natural solutions to clearing toxic waste. You will use technology to improve the total balance of your planet.

Yes, in many ways it will be a return to nature, with technology facilitating a deeper and grander understanding of the way nature functions, and how humanity can function in harmony with it. So there will be co-operation, a harmonising and a blending together of particular types of technology which will be beneficial. Bringing your lives gradually back into harmony with nature will cause a major leap forward. Then technology will take on a different expression altogether! Do not be overly concerned, as some have indicated, that you will wake up one day to find nothing works any more; that you cannot use your refrigerator or your vacuum cleaner! "What will I do? I cannot clean the house or wash the clothes! I will have to use my hands!" It will not be quite like that! Changes, yes, but changes that will be in harmony with the environmental concerns.

There is much that cannot be brought forth at this time because there has not been a firming up of those consensus beliefs which have been put in place in the fifth-dimensional world. The fifth-dimensional world is the realm of imagination. Many place it outside of themselves as if it is a place to which you are going to travel. Let us remind you yet again. You are multi-dimensional beings. *You exist on all dimensions at the same time.* Your task is simply to expand your consciousness beyond the veils you have placed around you, in some cases as hard as the shell of an egg, and begin to use the faculties which are part of the higher dimensions. Imagination is the faculty of the fifth dimension. It both enables you to image and to hold the images you have created so that you can ultimately move *into* them. Already the new world is taking shape on the fifth dimension. As the old world breaks down you will gradually move into the new.

Can you imagine the chicken deciding that all that exists is what it is able to see inside its shell and decide to stay there? Nature deems otherwise and provides an instinctive response to release the chicken from the egg. In a similar way your own instinctive response is being activated and you are all working your way out of your own shells. You have probably heard the idea that whatever you think comes about for you. You will say: "Yes, but I think many things and they don't always come about." Just wait until you get to your future! It is all waiting for you in varying ways. You might say: "I want my motor car now", but you forgot to put in a few little clauses. You forgot to read the fine print and you will go forward and it may not be until next year or the year after that the motor car comes along. You will wonder why and it is because you forgot to put in a few little clauses. Or perhaps you put in a condition or two such as, "when I work hard enough", or "when I feel deserving". Already those blueprints for your future are taking shape in the fifth-dimensional worlds. Then, as you usher yourself forward, you will suddenly burst through and "Oh, there is this wonderful place! How did it get there?" Well, you put it there and you have been putting it there for quite some time now. You are the creators of your future, and you are actually creating a new world for yourselves, more than you realise.

It is as very exciting world. As we perceive it at this time, we can very happily sit back and say: "Thank Goodness, oh, thank Goodness. We thought a few years ago that you would not make it. You have proven us wrong! You have proven to be very worthy of your abilities as co-creators." At this point of time you are not able to see what you are creating, but we assure you that when you do see it, you will be pleased. This is not to say that you have finished it yet! You have not quite put the 'paint on the walls'. You have not quite 'put the carpets in the rooms'. We are using analogies here. This is what is taking place in those realms where the thoughts are moving forward and become a part of your future and you are moving towards that. It is a most exciting period of time. The technology of the mind and the imagination will ultimately become the primary technology, for the power of the mind to bring about change will be realised by many. While an external technology is moving through its changes, so too is the application of the technology of the mind. We will discuss these at length at another time.

Question: How will the education system change?

Education at this period of time, whether primary, secondary or tertiary, is usually in a classroom setting. A teacher standing before a class of students has proven to be an inappropriate way of learning for many students who are not as left brained as their contemporaries. In the years ahead there will be a shifting and a changing in the activation of the right brain, the imaging brain, the visualising brain, the brain that has to do with being able to 'see beyond'.

Now, regarding television and video programs, there will be much use of classroom situations where there is the television in the classroom. At the same time there will be computer-assisted classrooms where the television and the computer work in harmony together.

This will be in conjunction with activities in which the student, and this is the preliminary student, will be involved in specific exercises and activities, geared towards enabling the brain to develop in particular ways, so there can be self-generated exercises.

In the future, as we perceive it, each student will be given exercises related to changing what is actually on the computer screen without a keyboard! At the moment, you operate the computer via a keyboard. In the future, you will not need a keyboard. You will find the brain and its thoughts will create impulses. Initially, there will be certain headpieces - you are getting a little of this with virtual reality. Virtual reality will be an implement that will facilitate education. At the moment it is used as a game. In the future, it will be used as education. It will allow an activation of certain portions of the brain.

At the same time as this is taking place, realise that each of you has a subconscious mind. Your subconscious mind does not know the difference between what you actually imagine in your mind, and what literally takes place when you act it out in the physical body. You will find when you go into a scene that is virtual reality, as you imagine, as the brain is activated to perform certain skills, the mind expands according to what is taking place in the acting out on the screen.

Along with that, there will be further development in the areas of the arts, movement, dance and therapeutic physiological activation, so that the activation of the body will be utilised and combined with the imagination. What is experienced in the virtual reality will be acted out in the external world.

We would like to give you, if we may, a little of what is possible with virtual reality. The development in those areas has the potential to be able to go into the brain, to explore subconscious fears, subconscious past belief systems and subconscious memories which act as inhibitors causing certain restrictions and limitations in the individual. These can be projected onto a screen and the individual person is then able to flow through and handle and resolve those particular fears through the use of virtual reality.

Each person will find that there are no longer limitations and restrictions inhibiting his full potential, and each will be able to develop his fullest potential, in harmony with his own unique skills and the reasons why he has come into this lifetime in the first place. These will be exciting times. Many people will be frightened or concerned about these technologies: "What will it do to the brain? What will it do to the mind? It will feel as if it is out of control!" There will be grave concerns and many will say "You cannot do this. This is too dangerous."

Yet it has the potential to *heal* the physical body, to heal and change the very substrata of your genetic coding. It has the potential to bring about vast changes within the individual person. Those who have come to this planet with residuals from past life experiences and other planetary experiences will have the potential to heal those.

There is much which will bring the left and right hemispheres of the brain into harmony. They have been functioning slightly out of resonance with each other, causing a dissonance.

In the very near future, the left and right hemispheres will begin to come into synchronisation, and then there will be the awareness that the right brain already knows that everything is in harmony with All-That-Is. The left brain does not know that. So when the left brain is educated and brought into harmony with the right brain, there will be major leaps forward in the creative endeavours on your planet. Education will take on a vastly different role altogether and students will go through the education systems for longer periods of time because education will be seen as one of the primary benefits for all people. Instead of students leaving universities at nineteen years of age they may continue until thirty years of age, moving into their particular field of endeavour. There will be many, many exciting projects to come in the future. Do not fear your children will be confined to sitting at a computer desk looking at a television through eye pieces. That will be a part of it, but a small portion.

In the future, universities will be accessible to the child from around the age of thirteen years. Information is accessed and integrated faster than ever before and those who have been in the education systems will realise that it took you so many years to teach a child how to write in the past, and now only a very short period of time.

Because of the expansion of the brain and its increased ability to absorb information, each child will absorb *much* more information. So go forward and be willing to realise that yes, the right brain is going to be appreciated and valued. Your traditional IQ testing will no longer be used as a valid method of assessing a child's potential. Other more encompassing and accurate testing techniques will be used.

Question: How long do we have to wait for a new way of working?

There is the male energy and there is a female energy. The male energy is very action oriented, the female energy passive and receptive. Each is necessary in the discovery of new ways of being creative and expressive in the work force. We hear many people asking, what they are supposed to do, yet they do not realise that *they* are the ones who will tell themselves! It is through a process of discovery that new ways of expressions will come about.

You are not going to be spoon-fed any more. You have been children for too long. Now you are grown up. You are now the creators of your own reality. In that sense, waiting, yes, you are waiting on yourself. You are waiting until you realise what you are capable of doing. How do you discover that? Begin the process by using the male energy. Sit down and ask: "What do I like to do? What is it that I feel capable of doing? What would I like to explore, express, experience in the future? In what way would I like to be, yes, a hero, a warrior, a leader or an explorer. In what way do I wish to be a communicator or a healer?" These are the things you need to write down. As you write them, look for the response. Ask for the next stage of your journey. As you ask the question, the answers to your questions will appear right before your eyes! Yes, right there so you can hear them. Sometimes they will appear on television; sometimes when a friend comes to visit you; sometimes you will read the answer in the newspaper. Look around, watch, be aware. What you are supposed to be doing in your future will come *to* you and it will be right in front of you. Sometimes you will trip over it, so very close it is! "Oh, I didn't realise that this is what I was supposed to do!" Well, sometimes it is not the ultimate, but a stepping-stone in that direction.

The stepping stones lead you in the direction of your purpose and your destiny. You will not find the Grand Plan right there in front of you just yet! Step by step. Be willing to take the risk, to go one step at a time. Then, *follow the excitement!* It meanders this way and round that way, and being willing to go step by step by step, you will gain greater confidence and more will come to you. Suddenly you will find the thing that you were supposed to be doing is right there and you may even be doing it. Does this answer your question?

I am looking for the new technologies, the ways for me personally.

The new technologies are of your mind. They are the ways in which you learn to program and create what you desire to have in your life. Through the application of your choices and decisions, thoughts and feelings, beliefs and attitudes you become a master of creation. Through the tools of imagination, desire and expectancy you will create for yourself what is personally for you. No one else can tell you. It would take your power away. Your task is to discover how to apply the technology to create what you want. By applying the principle of resonance, and holding the resonance of your desire, you will attract to you what is in harmony with your desire. You live your desires, you express them in everything you do. Many will wonder how they could possibly desire cancer. *Cancer is created by the body as a solution to an underlying desire to escape from a situation that you may be experiencing as hopeless.* The same principle of resonance applies in the spiritual realms. If you desire to become more 'spiritual' - though we smile at this statement when we hear it because each of you is totally spiritual, even the beggar on the street - then we will suggest the following. All of the choices and decisions you make must be in total harmony with your belief in yourself as a spiritual being. You will live your life with all of the qualities that you know a spiritual person would have, such as love, integrity, self-worth, self-respect and a high self-esteem. You will have a very real sense of your personal power and be willing to express it. You will form loving and intimate relationships with your personal guides and your higher Self as well as those with whom you share your very personal life. You will dedicate time to yourself and your spiritual path, and sit in meditation and quiet contemplation and discover yourself and ultimately become a self-realised person.

By looking to the future, rather than to the past, you will attend to the present, and be aware of all that is coming to you in this present time. Listen to the voices of your friends. Listen to the messages and respond to them accordingly. These are the technologies you will use. As you respond to those, as you build that aura and resonance of success, love and prosperity around you, you will attract all the kindness, all the love and all the benefits that are appropriate for you in your spiritual journey.

Remember when you were children and the telephone was invented, and suddenly the telephone was in your home and your parents would not touch it. You, as the children, were more easily able to handle the telephone than your parents. Now your children are more easily able to handle the computers at this time. Even more, there will be a new generation of grandchildren who will more easily be able to accommodate not only your computers but the whole age of technology and the whole age of information. At the same time, they will be able to access a whole source of information from realms beyond the physical.

There is a direct relationship between the way information is accessed that comes via either the satellite or computer, and the way information is accessed from other dimensions. Those of you who have in some way resisted computers and fax machines and other newfangled gadgets will suddenly find that to be without them means it will be difficult to keep up. *All* of your letters will be sent by fax. You will find it so much easier to write a letter and put it through your fax. This will enable information to flow much faster. Everything will be much faster. In the same way, in your movement in the astral levels, you will be more easily able to attune and focus your mind to access and send information and to travel inter-dimensionally. The importance of focusing your mind will be seen as very important. While focusing your mind, you are also to bring in the emotions because it is a combination of emotion and thought. Together, the image that you are creating and the emotion, enable the creation of what you desire to manifest in your world.

Work

Moving beyond the old patterns of limitation, struggle and hardship, beyond the need for constraint and limitation as part of your life; you are moving into the early stages of a world where you will begin to see what you have always wanted and wished for - a world of peace and harmony. This will be a world where brother and sister of all nations may sit together, join together and understand each other.

The foundations are now being set in place, brick by brick. But these bricks are not of a kind you would see on the third dimension. They are the chains that link and bind together the ideas and the concepts, the visions and the dreams, the goals that each of you in your own mind and heart has been dreaming. Learning that all you have ever dreamed of, or ever wished for, could come true, could fill some of you with a certain degree of apprehension. Oh, what would you do without struggle? What would you do with all that extra time you exert in doing it the hard way, climbing the mountains on your knees? Oh yes, we see you having such joy in the struggle to receive pats on the back. "Haven't you done such a wonderful job! You have worked so hard! You deserve a reward for your hard work!"

Could you imagine receiving a reward without having to work for it? Would it mean as much to you? These are questions that you need to ask yourself, for you have developed a value system that is totally different from what you are moving towards in your future. "Oh yes, I deserve this. Look what I did for Mrs. Jones down the street! And look at what I did for charity. I deserve, because I have been such a good wife, such a good husband. I am entitled to these benefits."

We wish you to know that deservability based on entitlement is not necessarily the basis for rewards. There is now a loosening of the old ways of doing things and the reasons for doing them. These reasons will drop away, and you may be left feeling a little empty at times, especially those of you who have worked for reasons of entitlement or deservability. You will move into a new frame of reference that challenges you. You may suddenly feel lonely or insecure, doubting yourself because you only had value when you were working so hard, doing the right thing to please everyone.

It is time for you to change the reasons why you do what you do, to shift your vision beyond doing it for entitlement, or deservability that has a negative frame of reference, into a deservability that is one which involves dignity. This new frame of reference will change your emotional state. Depending on your choices you will move into either doubt, uncertainty, insecurity and loneliness, or into the feelings of joy, happiness, wonder, awe, excitement and pleasure.

If we were to ask you what your choice was, we know what you would prefer to have, yes! Begin even now to allow joy into your life, to experience the wonder of your creations, to move forward into an expansion of positive emotion. In this way you will create miracles where you receive, not because you have worked so hard or are entitled to, but *because you are who you are.* You will create miracles because of your ability to embrace a positive emotion. The transformation of yourself will begin in new and very exciting ways. You are beginning the process of change within your body, mind and brain.

Some of you may be in business, in a particular type of work that has been for the most part successful and pleasurable for quite some time. Now you find, for various reasons, the business is no longer working in the way it has been. Or, perhaps you are losing interest. It does not give the same degree of pleasure when you go to work in the mornings. You often find yourself feeling somewhat subdued and reticent about going in to work. The old ways are falling, falling, falling away. Many will find that what has been appropriate in the previous several years will no longer be appropriate.

It is your higher Self and those guiding influences around you endeavouring in their way to redirect you, to place you in a position where you will re-assess your life and your values and what is in harmony with your vision for your future.

The world in which you live is overlaid by many, many dimensions. In this very room there are beings who walk, stand, sit and have their expression of life, but in a different dimension altogether than the one in which you live. The only reason you are not able to perceive them is because the wavelength of your world's vibration is out of synchronicity and not in harmony with the world in which they express and live. Moving forward and accelerating your emotional state into the greater expressions of wonder, of hope, love, joy and excitement, will shift your vibrational frequency. You will change the wavelength in such a manner that you will be attuned to the higher frequencies of vibration. In this way, you will be able to perceive those who are definitely in the same time, but in a different space, of your world. Some would call it clairvoyance and clairaudience. You are moving toward being able to see and hear, to sense and to know that which is beyond the limitations of this particular wavelength.

The world is being quickened. Think of ice changing into water. By heating the ice, the crystalline shape of ice begins to break apart and the configuration changes so it becomes liquid. The molecules in your body, the crystalline shapes of the cellular brain that have enabled your brain to function in the way it has for such a long time, are beginning to change. The vibrations from the cosmic realms, higher levels of electromagnetic energy and solar radiations, are causing a quickening in such a manner that new brain pathways are being activated and you will begin to *see* because you will not have that bonding of those crystalline formations that have limited your perception. We wish you to realise through to 1998 there will be the breaking down of the bonds and the links that have been in the way of your awakening. After 1998, there will be linkages created in new ways.

Chapter XI
Time And Space

Creating Space
Beyond The Third Dimension
Imagination And Meditation
Future Lives
Causal Plane

CHAPTER ELEVEN

Time And Space

We wish to discuss with you the dynamic of time so you may appreciate that time is also moving through a process of change which will touch you in very profound ways. Your chromosomes and the genetic codes of your DNA have been created with time as a foundational principle. The process of growth from the child to the adult is based on a genetic program which unfolds with the passing of time. You have even programmed death into your DNA. Each stage of growth requires a degree of mastery over matter (the physical body) within the constraints of time and space.

Your third-dimensional world is recognised by the constraints and limitations of space, time, matter and energy. As spiritual beings you are continuously expressing yourself within the confines of these limitations. Only when you have mastered these specific limitations will you set yourself free to expand and express in the multi-dimensional universe.

Those who believe they do not have enough time are conforming to those limitations. So we encourage you to change that belief. You *have* enough time. You have *more* than enough time! Believe that time no longer needs to be a constraint and limitation. Time is there for you to utilise; to have more or less of it as you need it. Most of you are impatient. You want to do it faster: "Tell me more, faster, quicker. I want to learn as much as I can, as fast as I can. I want to go forward quickly." It is *you* who are commanding to let it happen faster, therefore, time, which is very compliant, says: "Well, obviously they want us to happen faster" and that is why you have the impression time is speeding up.

When you need to slow down, you can slow down as easily as you have been able to speed up. Time is an illusion and you have as much or as little as you need. The idea of time speeding up is a relative state based on your life becoming more intricate and complex with more information to integrate and more responsibilities. The illusion is you are doing more in what appears to be less time.

The veils between your conscious, subconscious and unconscious mind are gradually dissolving. The subconscious and unconscious mind have their expression in multiple time and space. Through these parts of your mind you have access to multiple dimensions. You may see how this is possible when you recall your dreams and have your out-of-body experiences. When you move astrally out of your bodies, you can be out there for what appears to be a very long period of time, what may even appear to be a week, but when you return to your bodies, it will be as if only half an hour has gone by. In the astral realms you find time has a very different component to it. We are telling you this so you may see what is perceived in your minds as time is beginning to break down to enable an expansion into fourth dimension and beyond, so you may view time and space in a differently.

In your present stage of growth it will take time to learn how to adjust to time as it is to be expressed in the multiple dimensions. Time is available to you as you require it. You can have as little or as much time as you need. When you need more time, you may adjust your thinking and allow there to be more time, and express and act and behave as if there is more time. If you would like less time, in the same manner, you may hasten time so there is less time between one experience and another.

The lesson for this is *always to remain in the present*, only the present. All you require will come to you, for realise now you are the very centre of the universe. You always have been. Everything you need will be there at the right and appropriate time. This has always been the case, but now you will become more aware of it. You will feel as if you do not have to push in order to make it happen. It will happen because it will be there for you at the right time.

There was a time in your past, in Lemuria certainly so, when you were not controlled by time, when the clock did not exist and you honoured the passing of the cycles of seasons. You respected the Goddess and her influence upon you. Relatively recently you entered a linear expression where you straightened out time and things were measured according to past, present and future. You began to give power to your past and to history. You forgot a very important premise: it is your vision and dream for the future which creates the present. You have decided to interpret your present based on your past and allowed your past to be the reason why you do not go forward.

Many of you are still locked into your old patterns of the wounded child. We are not attempting to take away from you the significance of those traumatic experiences, however, we do encourage you to see them for what they are. They are messages. You need to let go of the past as the cause preventing you from going forward into your future. It simply means you are allowing your past to control you. It is more important now to look to the future and ask yourself what experiences you anticipate. If you do not like what you see, you can change it. You have many potential futures. Why would you create one which is not full of everything that you would love to have in your life?

Each of you has entered into this lifetime with many potential futures. Your personal life and the future of your planet is dependent on your ability to maintain a vision and a goal that is in harmony with your preferred future, both for yourself and your world. That is the magic of the fourth dimension and beyond. Your task is to become a conscious creator of a new world.

As the veils are removed, so too, will time change and no longer be a constraining influence. In this third dimension, you are bound by time and, we might suggest, not for very much longer. For some of you, you are already experiencing the speed of your creative endeavours. *The time between the thought and the manifestation is shortening.* As you integrate into the fourth dimension and beyond, time will become your friend. It is less able to control you in the ways it has done before. You are here to be empowered by the right use of time. Those who understand how to work this time, will ultimately be able to take a journey which would normally take two hours in one to one and a half hours. How did you do it? You learnt the principle of time! You learnt time was not a controlling factor. You are the creator of the limitations and time is a limitation you have placed upon yourself by the very idea you do not have 'enough time' and that it takes a certain amount of time to do a certain task. You will learn very quickly, because you all say: "We are in a hurry. We want it to happen faster. We are impatient!" As you state that, you will bring back to you the requirement to learn the lessons faster, to address the issues of negative ego and shadow faster. When you wonder why it seems to be an avalanche, it is because you have said: "We are in a hurry. We wish to go forward *very* fast!"

One year will be contracted to three to four months of time. In the fourth-dimensional world, your concept of time begins to be altered. As you go beyond, into fifth and sixth dimensions, time as you know it ceases to exist and the thoughts you think manifest instantly. You, who are learning to master time are being taught how to think, how to create, how to manifest in such manner as is in harmony with your divine purpose. You are being shown with greater haste the mirrors and the feedback from your external world. You are being shown so very clearly that you are the creator of everything in your life. Some of you know that in principle, but have not learnt the truth within your hearts. As time collapses, you are being shown faster and faster the direct reflection of your beliefs.

As your planet is moving toward some of the most exciting, most dramatic, wondrous and beautiful events, you have the opportunity to create the magic and the miracles within your own personal lives. The tools are given to you to enable you to link with the fifth-dimensional levels where miracles can occur. The miracle occurs outside of time and space, outside of what 'ought' or 'ought not' to occur. In other words, many of you believe a miracle can only occur if the person is a magician and a believer in God and prays consistently.

All of you are being taught to be miracle-makers, magicians of the highest order. You are being taught to create miracles in your lives because a miracle can occur outside of time and outside of space. We will give you an illustration. You may find your bank balance is very much in the red. You have insufficient funds to pay the bill. They are about to repossess your car and the boss has just told you that your job is on the line. Would you love a miracle to occur?

When you are able to encompass fully the fifth-dimensional skill of creative imagination and utilise the skills of right choice and when you are able to change the negative beliefs into positive ones, then in an instant of time you can create your bank balance to be in the black. It is in those periods of time many people do pray and in the prayer create the miracle. The Ancient Ones knew prayer was a direct access to the fifth dimension, whereby it is possible to create something outside of the constraint of time and bring it into this world.

The spiritual laws take you into timelessness and there thought and manifestation occur at the very same time. By extending your vision into the fifth dimension, and by creating the solution in the vision, the desires and the dreams, you bring that solution down into this third-dimensional world, thus do you create the miracle. Suddenly you wake up and say: "I must have dreamt it. It was, I thought, a dream, but suddenly 'the problem' has been resolved."

Choose time to be your friend and affirm to yourself you have the time and you will create those opportunities which will be 'in' time, in this third-dimensional world. The miracles are originating up here, but they come down to manifest in time. For all of you who have made this decision to explore the ultimate of materiality, your final frontier is to understand the concept of time and space for they are the very things that bind you.

Creating space

Using the same analogy with space, to those of you who say: "I do not have the space", we will say you are a creator and you can create the space. The reason why many of you do not create the space is because in creating the space you need to be alone, and aloneness is so close to loneliness that you are afraid. Create the time and the space by realising you are the master of both. Set aside those periods of time where you are able to be in your own space. Be still. Be quiet. Be contemplative. Enter into that space. It is there that you will have that clear access to the source of the miracle. It is there that you will enable change to occur. It is there you will discover those of us who have our expression in a different space. As you access that space, you will be able to communicate with us.

Oh, Beloved Ones, you are so very close. See the beauty and the radiance of that which pours from you. Embrace your true soul that you might honour yourself and love yourself sufficiently. You are at present controlled, limited and imprisoned by the dimensional patterns which you have created for yourself - twelve by twelve dimensions. Some would say you are moving from the third to the fourth. On a broader scale you are moving from the third to the twelfth into a multi-dimensional world.

You are moving very, very rapidly. Many of you may be feeling overwhelmed by the pace of change, by the number of different activities in which you are caught up. You will find there is a feeling of too much happening too quickly. That is the time for you to go into your centre, for while you remain on the rim, you will only experience the feeling of speed. As you move into the centre, into the eye, you will again find your balance, enjoying the harmony within the timelessness. Now is the time to look at yourself very closely and discover what locks you to your past.

Beyond the third dimension

Question: Is the third dimension to remain, or will it be completely absorbed into the fourth?

We will explain. Imagine what the planet Mars looks like.

Barren.

Very barren, yes. You *see* Mars with third dimensional eyes. When *we* look at Mars, we see something very different. We see a place which is rich and beautiful, with streams, rivers and waterfalls.

It is a rich and inhabited planet on its other dimensions! In the same way your planet Earth will look barren on its third-dimensional expression. It will not be able to sustain life as you know life to be. The fourth, fifth and beyond dimensions will supersede it and will only be seen by those who have the eyes to see. The vision you hold of a world in imagination is the world into which you will move, and will become what you call the fifth-dimensional world. The third dimensional world will cease to exist as it is at this time.

We are saying something quite radical to you. The transitions you will experience will be transitions of ease. You will be moving through them with such a degree of consciousness, it will be as if at times you will hardly notice a ripple. You will feel as if suddenly the rivers are becoming clear, as if the trees are becoming taller and everything is more rich and fertile. And the colours you will see! You have never seen colour like that, *ever before*. You will experience the change of the plant and the animal kingdom. You will be changing together. You will be aware that the animal kingdom and the plant kingdom will shift consciousness in a most amazing way, and you will suddenly become aware you can talk to the animals!

Your levels of communication will depend on your love, the connections you have to your own emotion and also your ability to create clear images in your mind. Love is what will allow the greater link to form and that feeling of love will embrace all of life's expressions.

Be aware the changes which are taking place now are to occur even more rapidly, more powerfully and there is an acceleration towards the higher levels of the experience of love, of opening up intuitively, enabling you to tune into fourth-dimensional experiences. With the quickening of time, whatever you think will be created so much faster. It is now time for you to really be aware of the power of your own creative abilities. When you decide what you would like to experience, do it with clarity, with emotion and do it with all of the faculties that will enable it to come through without deviation.

Many of you are astrally projecting at night with a certain degree of awareness. Some of you surface in the mornings with a sense of having left your bodies. When you are leaving your bodies, some of you may find in the projected state you are able to move through the wall that is the third dimension. You leave your body and there you are in your bedroom. Or you may find yourself visiting a friend or a neighbour. This is all part of the astral world that exists beyond *and* within your third dimension.

Some of the other dimensional experiences are very different from your third-dimensional existence. You may move out of your body and into realities that are not in any way, shape or form connected to the third dimension. You may be moving into fourth or fifth dimensions and even beyond that. As you practise, circumstances will gently encourage you to take charge of your inter-dimensional travel.

In your present life you will be moving into the fourth dimension with your physical body. In the very near future each of you will experience very strong indicators of moving through the transition between the third and the fourth dimensions. You will feel a little disconcerted because of the strangeness and uncertainty. You will experience adjustments within your brain and may become confused. You may lose your way when you are driving your car. You may forget where you are. All of you will be going through the transition over the next twenty years. We will encourage you to stay awhile! Be not in a hurry to depart, because it will be an exciting period of time! The transitional stage is a learning stage. It will be like going into a completely new 'city'. It will not be like a city, for this is an analogy. It is like learning a new set of tools, learning to go down the streets in different ways, to travel around using different skills.

Question: When will we be in place in the fourth dimension?

You are basically straddling the dimensions between third and fourth. It is not a situation where on a given date or time everyone will move into the fourth dimension. Each person is embracing the fourth dimension at his own pace. It is not a place to which you go, but simply an expansion of awareness beyond the limitations of your present third-dimensional beliefs. It is possible for you to be fully in the fourth dimension right now.

Some of you are moving easily between those dimensions and can see beyond the veils and have no concern about being in third or fourth because you know you are living, as it were, very close to fourth-dimensional consciousness. We are reluctant to use the term 'hundredth monkey', as we prefer to use the term morphogenic resonance - but suffice it to say, once a certain number of people have achieved a certain level of awareness, it will make it easier for others to achieve that state of consciousness.

Question: I was told there will be three different waves of people being moved up - one hears all kinds of stories.

The three waves need to be understood in a different context. It is a fallacy of human consciousness to see things in such a literal context. The three waves indicated will occur over periods of time. You are currently moving through the first wave with many people moving through tragic and disastrous releases. These include wars, famine, disease and natural disasters. This is the first big wave.

The second wave will begin after the year 1998 and will concern that group of people who are not able to or have chosen not to remain conscious during the transition. Many will take their leave in a variety of different ways.

The third wave will consist of those people who have decided to remain conscious while the whole planet ascends. This will occur in approximately the year 2012. We do not suggest the planet is then going to ascend, but it is the time when time as you know it will cease to exist. That is the time when the Mayan calendar ceases and why no one has predicted anything beyond that time. Your world will be very different then, but not so dramatically different that you will have no reference points. You also will be very different, but you are also very different from the person you were ten years ago. It is just that the difference between now and that period of time will be quite dramatic.

And so, in the dimension we are moving into, my understanding is, that from that dimension we can see into the other dimensions. Is that correct?

We will use another analogy. If you are a fish and you are under the water, you are able to see relatively clearly under the water, yet you are not necessarily able to see beyond the water very clearly. Another very simple analogy may be the difference between the way a child is able to understand things compared to an adult.

A person who has clairvoyant and clairaudient abilities, even in your third-dimensional worlds, is able to see into the fourth dimension and also into the fifth. If you are physically blind, for you the world does not exist in the same way as it does for other people who are not blind. In a similar way, those who have activated their fourth-dimensional senses while they are still living in the third dimension are able to see and experience a very different world beyond the third dimension. They are able to see those beings who live their life in the other world, living and doing the things which are important to them. You do not have to go into the fourth dimension to see into other dimensions. You only need to develop a greater awareness by activating your higher-dimensional senses. Then you will be able to access all the dimensions consciously, even while you are still in the third dimension. In the process you will be increasing the vibrational frequency of your physical body to facilitate your ability to see and hear.

From the perspective of the higher-dimensional beings looking into your third-dimensional world, be aware that they do not see your body in the same way you do. They see your body as moving fields of colour similar to the way a clairvoyant would see your auric field.

We explain. You have a physical body that is akin to the mineral kingdom. You have an etheric body that is akin to the plant kingdom. You have your astral body or emotional body. You have also your mental body that enables you to be conscious. Your spiritual body connects you to the spiritual realms, those levels which are beyond the constraints of your physical world. In the usual circumstances, the process you call death enables you to move into the fourth dimension. You leave your physical body, and your astral, mental and spiritual bodies move to the higher levels, initially the astral realms to that level or overtone that resonates with the degree of your development.

218

Those who have succeeded in fulfilling their purpose in life and have transformed the negative patterns enabling the greater love to be experienced, will quickly move through the astral realms into the higher mental planes of the fifth dimension. This will be a familiar place for many of you because it is your idea of heaven.

Now you are paving the way to do it all in a different way. You are changing your vibrational frequency by releasing the negative patterns which prevent you from seeing beyond the veils *while you are still in your physical body.* Death will have a totally different meaning to you. You are drawing the higher worlds to you. While it may appear as if you are still in the third dimension, you are in fact expanding your awareness, so you hardly even notice everything is changing, including your ability to 'see', 'hear', and channel from your 'guides' which you now almost take for granted. Even five years ago much of this would have been beyond your conception. You are embracing the fourth dimension so easily you hardly know it is happening.

When you are able to see many others of the higher dimensions who are close to you, and communicate with them, then you will know you are close. When your life goes through dramatic changes and you are yearning to go back to nature and to live in harmony with natural laws, and when nothing else matters except your spiritual journey, and when you experience a love so great that your whole life is in total balance and harmony and you realise how easy it is to create miracles, then you will be on the threshold of that shift in consciousness, where you will know you are the master of matter and the third-dimension. Then will you transcend and become Christ conscious.

Having made the decision to participate in a major shift in consciousness, you are being observed by those who are not in a third-dimensional physical form. Many are there to support you, others are curious how you will achieve such a phenomenal task and yet others in their own way attempt to sabotage. Do not be concerned about them, as those light beings from the higher realms will assist you to overcome any force which may be applied against you. They are aware your progress will benefit the whole universal matrix.

219

Each of you has made the decision to participate at this time. Have you ever wondered why so many have been born at this time? More than five billion of you! Five billion, multiplying at a rapid rate, moving towards ten billion by the end of your decade. What is to become of you? So many are seeking to participate in this grand event, something that has never, ever been allowed before in the entire history of the universe. Something that has never, ever been considered possible before. You have decided to ascend consciously. You do not fully appreciate what that means as yet. You are still constrained by the limitation of the third-dimensional consciousness. We are planting seeds in your consciousness to prepare you for the changes so you may begin to blend with the idea and feel your way through the years to come.

Question: I have been told that in the year 2012 we will go into fourth dimension. Some say we could be there as early as 2005.

Each person is an individual in his own right. There are those who very easily stand in both worlds. You have access to fourth dimension and beyond. It is not something that will occur, being one day in the third dimension, the next day in the fourth. The dimensional levels are overlaid one on top of the other. The only differentiation is a change in vibrational frequency. Each dimension is a hologram of all of the dimensions. It is possible to access all dimensions through every dimension. You only need to know the keys, symbols or sounds which open the doors to that dimension.

Many of you will understand the concept of cloning. Your scientists are realising it is possible to take the genetic material from a cell and reproduce the whole body which will be an exact replica of its original source. The psychic is able to hold an article of jewellery and through psychometry attune to the owner and pick up much that has happened in that person's life and even in previous life experiences. In each particle of information, the totality of all information is available. Your universe is a hologram. You have your life in one very small portion of it, but you have access to all of it. Within each and every cell of your body, there is *all* - physical, emotional, astral, etheric, mental and spiritual - through all and every dimension. Each cell in your body is an antenna for the entire universe. It is a hologram. So to say in a particular year that you as an individual will move into the fourth dimension is simplifying the idea too much. In your world it could happen tomorrow or it may be a gradual transition to enable the ease of adjustment.

Imagination and meditation

Practise imagination, practise imaging, for in that way you exercise those portions of your brain which are necessary for you to move forward into the higher-dimensional awareness. If we had given you a pen at the age of thirty-five and asked you to write a letter, and you had never been through elementary school and never learned the alphabet or how to read and write, you would have great difficulty in writing a letter. Using your imagination is like learning your A-B-C. Imagination in your preliminary stages is necessary for you to be able to, in the future, image, to make it real and then step into the image. You will become magicians through the ability to image. Tesla knew the power of imagination. He created working models in his mind of all of these experiments before he created the prototype.

Through the use of imagination you can create visual scenes similar to your ideal world. By activating all of your senses in the inner world scene, you are preparing those senses to function in the other dimensions. This also prepares the way to communicate telepathically with each other, to communicate with the animals, with the Earth and the plant kingdom. Imagination is the A-B-C. Practise it in all of your meditations. Visualise, and as you visualise, every image will become more and more real. We do encourage you to do this, for your world will surely change. You will always initially perceive us through your imagination. We like to use your imagination so you can have a sense of what we look like, and then, as you move beyond, because you have mastered it, we will appear to you as we truly are, and you will be very much aware that the veils have surely dissolved.

Some of us live in a world that is similar to yours. We do not have motor cars, television sets or air-conditioning. We have learned how to adjust our body temperatures. We have learned how to find the information we need without televisions and telephones. We do not need computers either. Were you to walk out into the country amongst our trees and watch the flowing streams, you would see the similarities, except our streams flow swiftly, cleanly and brightly. They sparkle with a life of their own. Our trees live life in their fullness and certainly expound their true colours. Even as the birds fly in the sky, they do demonstrate the beauty of their colours, for their feathers are of a kind which demonstrate the beauty of their souls.

We manifest in robes of many colours. You know the story of Joseph and his coat of many colours. It was not a physical garment they were talking about. It was his auric field. It was of many colours, and those who saw him were able to see with their true eyes the beauty of the soul that this man was, a highly evolved soul with his coat of many colours. You too, with your radiance of colours will surely find yourself glowing in a different way. You have come into this life to change your vibration, to change your garment, to remove what is inhibiting so you can be the vehicle that expresses your true radiance.

Many of you may experience a feeling of not being in your bodies, feeling as if you are banging into the walls, or of not driving your car in a sensible manner. Be aware when your co-ordination is slightly out and you feel disoriented. This is the time to stop and centre yourself and enter the stillness. It is most important that you remain in your body during these times of transition. This is not a time to escape or separate from the physical body.

If you go through the transition feeling as if you are not able to accommodate the increased energies, it may cause headaches, eye strain, or certain weaknesses in your body. These are the times to spend in meditation, and to begin the process of activating the brain. Realise that your brain is somewhat like an unused muscle. It needs to be exercised, by using imagination. So we ask you to sit in meditation and use your imagination.

It is now necessary for you to create images that can be as real as what you would consider to be real in your third dimension. Create an image where, if you take hold of a peach or an apple and you bite into it, the taste is as real as if you were eating it in third dimension. If you imagine standing with your feet in the ocean, feel the water around your feet as if you were really there. You will need to exercise all of your senses. In your imagination you are preparing yourself for the fifth dimension which is created from imagination!

Future lives

A specific configuration of planets within your solar system and beyond it will provide the necessary elements to accelerate the change in your brain. Chemical activity will cause the release of specific neurotransmitters that have the task of accelerating change above and beyond what has been normal within the human brain. The awakened pineal gland will release a drop, like a dew drop on a flower petal. That drop will gently fall down into the pituitary gland and create an explosion therein. It will cause a reverberation in your brain which will create a harmonic that will cause all the cells in your body to awaken. That harmonic also will release yet another drop, like an elixir, which will then pour down into the thyroid and again into the vessel of your heart.

Many will wonder why they can suddenly access those other lifetimes. Well, because they are in your body. They are *you*. You are not separated from those other lifetime experiences. You are living them all at the same time! It will depend on what you are experiencing at any given point of time and where your focus is, as to which life flows into your consciousness.

And while we speak of past-life experiences to be experienced in the present, we may also say that the you that you are now is also connecting to the future you's! You have many future you's. You did not just decide to have one future, you have many choices. You decided on a number of possible futures and you sent yourself out there through the labyrinth of possible choices so that you would see which one would be the best choice. In making those choices, you activated this one, to bring it forward into your present life experience. You are now bringing your future into your present, as you have previously been bringing your past into your present. Your future lifetimes will indicate the potentials you are facing within yourself: how great you can be, how expansive, powerful, beautiful and wise you can be. It is a very different perspective from trying to resolve the problems of the past.

If you are afraid of your future because it seems threatening, choose a different future! Why do you choose a possible future that seems threatening when you are now the miracle-maker who can create a future which will support you?

Your future life is looking at you, your trauma and the ways in which you limit yourself, calling out to you to blend with it. You may allow your future to be your present now. Because many of you still hold the idea that this is impossible, you maintain a planet that mirrors to you war and battle, hunger and pain, terrorism and violence. It is time to realise that in the power toward which you are moving, you can step into your capabilities and bring about the change *instantly*. Your future and your mind have the capability to bring about such powerful transformations throughout your planet that one of the futures of your planet can be a total eradication of all violence.

Causal plane

When you wake up from your night-time dreams, you may recall having been in a strange place talking to people who were not quite like humans. Some of you may have felt you had been there before, as if it were a familiar place. There is such a place that is familiar to you as you travel in the external astral realms. There is a place that is like home. We describe it as being on the fifth dimension, and we might call it the wayside station because it has been set aside for humanity to heal itself and prepare for the next sojourn into a physical form.

You will return there between each of your life experiences. When you have completed the need to incarnate, you are able to move beyond the fifth dimension.

All who choose to die to this physical body will move through the fourth dimension to that place you call heaven. Oh yes, there *is* a heaven and it is that particular place you call the fifth dimension. All of you know it well for you always go there between your lifetimes. Many of you will find you also go there when you are in a state of stress or distress and when you need to be rejuvenated or reminded of your purpose and reason for coming to this planet.

It is a very harmonious place with colours very different from the Earth colours. The colours, fragrances and music are unique and yet known to your heart and soul. All of you will access that dimensional experience with greater degrees of awareness, being able to consciously decide to go there. For this is what we also call the causal level. There you can create miracles. *There, as you think so it is!*

Chapter XII
Destiny
And The Love Of Goddess

CHAPTER TWELVE

Destiny And The Love Of Goddess

We have been sharing with you at length for quite some time. Now we wish to discuss with you the power of love. Many have a romantic idea of love. While we do not undervalue the love you have with the most intimate and special person in your life, we would like to expand the idea of love so you may begin to see it as one of the most important of all your experiences.

Love is more than an emotion. It is the only energy which will take you from where you are to the highest dimensional levels in your universe and beyond. Love opens all doors, removes all fears, claims all wisdom and empowers to act in all situations. Love unites with true understanding. With love you honour and respect, and give value to Self and others. When each of you is able to love and be loved by Self and others in all fullness, you will know you have access to all resources. Love denies nothing and provides everything including wisdom and the right use of power. *When you love absolutely, all of your needs are met.*

In your distant past in the times of early Lemuria you had been genetically manipulated. You were separated from the source of love, from the love of God/Goddess. Fear was programmed into your DNA. The feeling of separation has been with you since that time. Each of you may feel you are unique, because you feel all alone and no one understands your feelings of separation and sense of difference. You do not realise, *each of you feels the same way.* Every time you are born, that separation is reinstated when your umbilical cord is cut. It is emphasised, yet again, when there are even more periods of separation from either one or both of your parents.

These periods of separation are interpreted as abandonment, betrayal, or rejection. They sometimes leave you with feelings of shame or humiliation. Your own interpretation may be the specific trauma you have come to heal in your present life experience. The same feelings of betrayal may have originated from the very beginning, as far back as Atlantis or Lemuria and continued to be imprinted upon you lifetime after lifetime until you decided you had to overcome. There are two levels of these traumas around love, which we wish to discuss with you.

One is at the level of the human experience. The abandonment, betrayal, shame, rejection or humiliation may have originated from a specific experience of love. Perhaps you were about to marry and your lover rejected you for another at the last minute. There are as many possible scenarios as there are people in the world. Your experience is specific to you and the drama in each life time will be very similar. Incest is a form of betrayal, shame or humiliation. Within the same experience, the child may feel humiliated and betrayed by the perpetrator and feel abandoned, rejected or let down by the only other person it felt it could trust.

The second level of trauma around love is specific to your relationship to God/Goddess. We are more particularly concerned about the love of Goddess for she is the one most accused of betrayal and abandonment. We will explain. All of you at some time in your many lives have lived within the confines of a temple, monastery or abbey. At other times, your deep religious conviction and worship of God/ Goddess or the gods, provided a level of safety and trust while you provided adequate sacrifices. When something happened to destroy that trust, such as a natural disaster, war or famine, your prayers and sacrifices were to no avail; or you were accused of being a witch. You were accused of being against the Church of God, and you did not understand. They attacked you. They tortured you. They destroyed you, and amongst all of that, you called out for God/Goddess and said: "Why are you allowing this to happen? Why do you not come to my rescue? Have I done something wrong? Did I fail you?"

Because of those experiences there was confusion, rage and anger, there was betrayal and the betrayed and you turned your back on God/Goddess. Your heart closed and your soul wept and went into hibernation. You, who have been betrayed in this lifetime, who have experienced that loss of soul, will find an aching within your heart and want to reach out for something. It is amorphous, not quite there, and you realise what you are seeking is what you had turned your back on, or you felt that Goddess had turned her back and abandoned you.

Your God or Goddess did not come to your rescue. There are many examples, when God/Goddess has failed you throughout your many lives. Many of you were burned at the stake, died as Christians when thrown to the lions, died in a dungeon after torture for a cause that was dear to your heart, or in some other way died a martyr expecting to be rescued by a miracle. Those experiences have left a deep scar in your heart and soul. Your soul, in some cases, has even separated from you because the pain was so great.

Now beloved ones, it is time to heal the wound, to remove the scar and begin to trust again. You may ask for a guarantee not to be hurt again. We would like to remind you, you are now more sophisticated. You have come of age. You are now able to embrace the truth. You create it all. You have always done so. Now that you are consciously aware of that principle, you can surely trust yourself not to create an experience that is not for your highest good. All of your experiences, including your relationships, are specifically designed to reveal the blockages which still need to be cleared. Use the affirmation: 'All of my relationships are healing relationships'. In this way, while experiencing your relationships, you trust your own inner guidance.

When you are able to recognise the belief which holds you locked into an old pattern, you are able to change it and release yourself from the control of the past. It is no longer appropriate to blame your past life, your parents, the school teacher or any other person you hold responsible for your so-called trauma. While Goddess has never really abandoned you, you have kept yourself cocooned within your own walls of protection, preventing Her love from reaching you. You maintain your isolation, wear a mask to hide your hurt and pain, and live your life on the surface, too afraid to dive deeply into the levels of intimacy which are needed for you to move beyond your limitation.

Many of you state you are in a hurry and you want it all now, however, we still see you hiding behind your veils of self-protection. You have created a body of flesh and bone and covered it with skin. The closest many of you will get to intimacy is through the sexual act. In the blending of vital fluids and the degree of union experienced with your body blending with another, you enter into a state of ecstasy culminating in an orgasm, which is the closest you will experience on your world to anything that even slightly resembles love in our dimension. Even the most profound of all of your orgasms can only be compared to a pat on the shoulder. In the dimensions of our vibration we blend the totality of our being when we express our love for each other. There are no secrets and we are totally known to each other on all of our levels. *We withhold nothing and give everything.*

Before you can go home you will each need to face your greatest fear. That is the fear of not being loved. You are now being challenged to be a receiver. Many refuse love. You do not wish to feel gratitude. You do not feel you deserve or have worked hard enough.

If any of you are in debt, you may be assured that you have not yet learned to be a receiver. You may see indicators of denying yourself when you have only a little money left over and another bill comes in or the car breaks down. These are the ways in which you prevent yourself from receiving for yourself. You will always find the way to do for another, but will leave yourself short.

Goddess is calling you. Your task is to respond to her call. It is her gift to you. Many of you will have difficulty receiving her gift. You have been taught throughout your life that it is better to give than to receive. May we suggest that until you are ready to receive the gift of love and light from Goddess you will prevent yourself from changing the fear-based DNA. Many of you will face varying degrees of fear, through to anxiety, terror and dread, to pressure you to reach out for help so the old patterns may be healed. The love and light of God/ Goddess is coming into your consciousness in a way that it has not for thousands of years. It will touch you in ways that will enable the following to take place.

Firstly, the Goddess energy will change your perspective of time and space. Your attention will be directed to purpose and destiny and you will begin to put your attention to your future rather than the past.

So many of you have been dedicated and committed to your personal growth and healing for quite a number of years: some of you five years, some of you ten or even twenty. You have been dedicated to healing yourself - to healing your soul, your psyche, your physical body, healing those negative beliefs and healing *all* of those experiences that are connected to your past lives or early present life. To that end, you have been motivated by the influences from your past. These influences have been very dramatic in many ways, especially for those of you who have been resolving and healing the idea of being the victim, or the martyr, or feeling as if you are powerless. These particular patterns, along with the shame, the blame, the lack of trust and many others, all have their connection to the past.

From this time on, the past will no longer have the same controlling influence over you. It is only your desire to continue to keep the past alive that reactivates the old wounds. We wish to state that anything that is residual, to which you feel inclined to say: "It must be because of that past lifetime" or "It must be because of the way in which my mother or father treated me as a child", know that this year is the turning point. Now, the motivating force is your future.

The second change that will become very evident with the influence of God/Goddess will be the changes within your physical body. Old genetic codes that cause ageing and death are being substituted by new codes enabling the body to stay younger longer, and ultimately to transcend the physical limitations. The neurotransmitters are releasing chemicals that have the components of the fountain of youth. Each of you who opens more to love will begin to glow. It will be as if the cells in your body show their true nature, that of the light within.

Thirdly, a process is beginning that will take some considerable time to complete and will enable the physical body to change its shape and form completely to become a light body. When you have achieved this state of consciousness you will be able to travel in your light body at will. You will have mastered the physical world. The light and love of God/Goddess will enable all of your blockages to clear with ease. The veils of fear, separation and loneliness will be replaced by a very real feeling of Oneness with your spiritual family, with your higher Self and with God/Goddess, All-That-Is. You may even feel drawn to surround yourself with like-minded people who share a common goal. Do not confuse this with the old concept of communes, where each person was seeking to act out his own negative ego. These new spiritually-based groups will recognise the strengths and weaknesses and work within those parameters.

The love and light of Goddess will also be experienced in the breaking down of all of the old patterns in the outer world which belong to the past. Her love will be present in establishing new solutions which are in harmony with a world that is yet to be born. Her love is also present and is strengthening in all areas of conflict in your world. You will see sabotage from time to time by those who seek to maintain the old patterns, however, the power of God/Goddess will be increasingly felt throughout your world. Initially, and for a few years to come, it will be felt as the labour before the birth. You will still see the signs which indicate her light and love flowing into the hearts and souls of all of humanity without exception.

You do not need to earn the right to be loved. You are loved totally and completely for who you are. You do not need to do anything. There is no *earning* in love. You *deserve* to be loved. It is your right and it is *now* that you need to be willing to be loved. If you *persist* in refusing to be loved, you will create for yourself many disasters in your life. It is for you to realise the power of the Goddess pouring down upon you, pouring down upon the whole of your world.

The Goddess is also working with your dreams, in ways you have not conceived of before. The God/Goddess is here to open a level of awareness, which will assist you to realise your dream life is your real life. The veils between your waking consciousness and your experience at night when asleep, will begin to disintegrate, and you will feel, over the period of the next several years, that you are requiring less and less sleep, and the sleep will be more akin to dreaming consciously. You will be encouraged by the God/Goddess energy to open the way to the dream. We shall expand a little more on the dream.

You have learnt about the value of imagination. You will now realise the impact you may personally have in creating your own dreams. You will enable your dreams to become manifest. You will become a conscious traveller in your own dream state. Conscious dreaming will prepare you for the greater impact of the Goddess energy. It is through the God/Goddess energy that you will learn you *are* a creator, in a very powerful and significant way! You need to be able to see clearly, for during next year (1997) you will be called to create your visions for your future and only when you can see clearly now, will your visions take shape.

Be aware, your dream will become real to the degree to which you harmonise with your purpose and destiny. These are positive dreams, which involve forming a deep and meaningful relationship with *all of life*. That means the planet itself, the birds, the animals, the trees - all of life. Remember, now you are opening up your senses so you can see beyond this world into the dream world and the dream world is where you see the life forms which give the vitality to the plants - the nature spirits. You will be able to see angelic beings, your guides and your counsellors. You will be able to see the extraterrestrials who are all around you. The great significance of this period of time now, is the Goddess energy pouring in so strongly through the Sirius vortex. It is a rebirth and a transformation. This is the time when the vortex that was closed over 90,000 years ago has been opened again.

Everything is in order for all of the light bearers to start waking up. This is the wake-up call! Those who are the light bearers were present at the time of the closing of the vortex. You have returned again to reawaken the light and love of God/Goddess within your hearts and souls. The Age of Aquarius is the Age of the Water Bearer. Each Age is approximately 2,160 years long. The Water Bearer will be pouring the spiritual waters from the higher dimensions in the outer world throughout the Aquarian Age. The light and love of God/Goddess

235

through the Sirius vortex will assist you to create a new spirituality. This will not have the undercurrents of religion, dogma and creed. Your task is to discover your own spirituality as you would most prefer to express it.

This is a period of time, when the God/Goddess energy touches you more deeply than ever before, establishing your connections to 'beyond this plane' stronger than ever before. A new form of spirituality will embrace your own individual way of expressing your spiritual Self. It will not be necessary for you go to church and pray on bended knees to Almighty God. Your new spirituality will take you beyond your present idea of God/Goddess, the All-That-Is. May we take you back to the beginning time - the time of original separation when the desire to have joy, to experience and to create, was the impulse that caused the original explosion from the source of love. The desire to relate, to create and to find the richness of Self reflected in the other, was paramount. Your new spirituality will remind you of that original purpose for which you initially entered into this universe. In your new world you will experience depths and heights of joy, expressed through the desire to create and relate, unimaginable to your present mind.

With fear no longer part of your nature, your resonant vibration will lift you into multidimensional levels of awareness. You will not see the human form, but the radiant beauty of the soul's true essence. All living forms will be seen in their true garments. Your rivers will glisten; your birds will reveal colour beyond physical perception and at last your trees and flowers will communicate with you. There will be no separation between any life form. The statement 'All is One' will be felt by the heart and soul.

You will discover the truth of the proclamation 'there is no time'. Your world will simply be, eternally, the external expression of your new radiant Self complete with a richness and vibrancy of colour. All around you will reflect the complexity of the holographic universe. It will be as if your world was transported into a completely new part of the galaxy. In truth, it will be a transportation of a different kind. You

236

are not going anywhere. You are simply becoming your truth and, in becoming, you will expand your awareness into the multiplicity of possible expressions.

The congruency of your personal choices at this period in your life will create the new Garden of Eden where all live in harmony: this time, not a garden that was created for you, but one that is created by you. This is indeed the Promised Land.

About The Author

Wendy Munro is a practising psychologist and psychotherapist. She gives seminars and workshops in metaphysics and spiritual development. Wendy is a natural clairvoyant and has been channelling for over twenty years. After travelling the world extensively she now resides in Western Australia.

P'TAAH - TRANSFORMATION OF THE SPECIES
channelled by Jani King

In an evermore troubled world, P'taah's message creates a light beacon signalling the end of humanity's long tunnel of darkness, leading it into light and joy.

Excerpt: 'You will come into concepts beyond imagination. When you come into the knowing that there is no separation of anything, then indeed you will change the universe: grand times of illumination, until there will be no time when you will not know that you are truly God.

When that time comes, beloved ones, your planet will reflect lights beyond imaginings - rainbow hues dancing like a fireworks display to light up the galaxies. The planet indeed will be a reflection of the GOD I AM.'

ISBN: 0 646 13606 2, size A5, 252 pages, soft cover.

ST. GERMAIN - EARTH'S BIRTH CHANGES
channelled by Azena

The upheavals, the unrest and torment within humanity at this time are the contractions and labour pains heralding a birth of an incomprehensible, cosmic magnitude. Earth and her children, in unison with the solar system and thousands of galaxies, are birthing into a new dimension. From the shores of eternal being, from the Council of Light, comes one called St. Germain to assist in this birthing process. As he bares his heart in love and compassion, rekindling an ancient memory, he transforms the prophecies of Old, of looming calamities and trepidation, into shining, new horizons without circumference. His gift to us is not approximate statement, but the promise of fact: freedom for humanity.

ISBN: 0 646 21388 1, size A5, 280 pages, soft cover.

ST. GERMAIN - TWIN SOULS & SOULMATES

channelled by Claire Heartsong and Azena

'Experiencing Christ-consciousness within yourself, loving unconditionally that which you are as you exist and abide in your reality at this point in time, creates the resonance within your being which attracts the identical essence within the opposite body of soul energy - your soulmate will manifest in physicality as a natural progression and merges with your energy and you with it. And as you merge together closer and closer and drink more and more of one another's cup, you become One, and you become one another's strength and one another's love. As this occurs, you experience what is called enlightenment.

When you experience this alignment and attunement with the All That Is, the physical expression of your soulmate automatically appears. And if you will recognize that you already embody the principle of love, then you will merge with your soulmate and the merging of soulmates creates miracles.'

ISBN: 0 646 21150 1, size A5, 160 pages, soft cover.

GARDEN OF GODS

by Peter O. Erbe

From the author of the highly acclaimed spiritual classic 'GOD I AM', comes 'GARDEN OF GODS', a deeply inspired collection of wisdoms, presented in the form of an 'open at any page' book, which may serve as a daily companion, offering profound insights.

Excerpt: 'For ere so long have you wandered the wilderness of your own making. Deep has been the grief of your perceived separation and heavy the ache within your heart longing for home. You are the traveller who journeyed distant lands and, thirsty and spent, beholds from afar a window in the night with candles alight, beckoning, and knows with trembling heart his kin await him with open loving arms; and no greater the anguish of his yearning than in this final hour before his return.

Take comfort then - for truly, the journey is but over. As in the blink of an eye shall you awaken and naught shall remain but the fleeting memory of an impossible dream.'

ISBN: 0 9586707 0 6, size 11.5 x 17.5 cm, 165 pages, soft cover.

IT IS NEVER TOO LATE
Astounding Life After Death Communications
by Anne Goodall

After his departure from this earthly plane, Mark begins to communicate with his wife Anne from beyond the veil. The resulting conversations will keep the reader enthralled, to say the least.

Excerpt: "Death is not the closing of a door emblazoned with the words 'It is too late.' It is an open pathway to a greater understanding, forgiveness and an opportunity for a further and happier life - life here and life there. Here and there are not even a breath apart and are inextricably bound together.

Death is just going through to the real life, something to look forward to. Death is really living. In other words, life is as death, and death is the real living."

ISBN: 0 9586707 1 4, size 11.5 x 17.5 cm, 140 pages, soft cover.